CONSERVING SWALLOWS

Conserving Swallows

Threats and Strategies for Different Species

MACK RAFEAL

Mohammed Altaf Hussain

CONTENTS

INDEX

INTRODUCTION

The universe of avian miracles is embellished by the smooth and gymnastic trip of swallows, a gathering of birds that has long caught the interest of the two ornithologists and devotees. Swallows are not simply elevated entertainers; they assume a fundamental part in keeping up with biological equilibrium by adding to bother control and going about as signs of ecological wellbeing. Notwithstanding, the actual presence of these striking species is compromised by a heap of difficulties, going from environment misfortune and environmental change to contamination and human obstruction. This perplexing embroidery of dangers requires a far reaching assessment of protection techniques custom-made to the different types of swallows tracked down across the globe.

The Puzzling Universe of Swallows:

Swallows have a place with the family Hirundinidae, incorporating north of 80 species internationally. These birds are described by their smooth bodies, pointed wings, and shocking ethereal deftness. Their transient examples, multifaceted settling ways of behaving, and consonant tweets have started logical interest and social importance over the entire course of time. Swallows are disseminated across many territories, from open fields and prairies to metropolitan conditions and beach front districts, adjusting to different environments with amazing flexibility.

The Danger Scene: Unwinding Difficulties to Swallow Populaces:

In spite of their flexibility, swallows face a raising cluster of dangers that risk their populaces around the world. One of the principal challenges is natural surroundings misfortune, as urbanization, farming extension, and deforestation infringe upon their settling locales. Environmental change presents extra intricacies, modifying the timing and accessibility of bug prey, upsetting relocation designs, and influencing the sensitive equilibrium of biological systems. Pesticide use and contamination further undermine their wellbeing and conceptive achievement, raising worries about the drawn out practicality of swallow populaces.

Species-Explicit Difficulties: Fitting Protection Approaches:

The assorted scope of swallow species across landmasses delivers species-explicit difficulties, requiring nuanced and custom-made protection draws near. For example, the Purple Martin (Progne subis) faces living space misfortune because of the downfall of appropriate settling locales, especially normal tree cavities. The Bluff Swallow (Petrochelidon pyrrhonota), known for its trademark gourd-molded homes, battles with adjusted bug accessibility brought about by rural changes.

In Europe, the Normal House Martin (Delichon urbicum) wrestles with living space misfortune exacerbated by changing structure practices and environment prompted modifications in bug overflow. Likewise, the Stable Swallow (Hirundo rustica), a recognizable sight across North America and Europe, faces difficulties connected with the accessibility of mud for home development, a basic part of their remarkable settling conduct.

In the Southern Side of the equator, the Welcome Swallow (Hirundo neoxena) faces environment debasement because of horticultural escalation, influencing its rearing achievement and populace elements. These shifting difficulties highlight the requirement for an animal groups explicit preservation approach that considers the complexities of each swallow species' science, conduct, and living space necessities.

Worldwide Viewpoints on Swallow Protection: A Mosaic of Systems:

The mosaic of swallow species disseminated across mainlands requests a worldwide viewpoint on protection, where cooperative endeavors rise above topographical limits. Different nations and areas have carried out assorted systems to address the dangers looked by their neighborhood swallow populaces.

In North America, drives center around safeguarding normal settling destinations, advancing the establishment of fake home boxes, and bringing issues to light about the significance of Horse shelter Swallows and Tree Swallows in bother control. European protection endeavors frequently include natural surroundings rebuilding, with an accentuation on safeguarding conventional settling destinations for species like the House Martin. In Australia, protection drives for species like the Welcome Swallow focus on alleviating the effects of land-use change and environment corruption.

Methodologies for Natural surroundings Conservation and Reclamation:

Natural surroundings protection and rebuilding structure the bedrock of swallow preservation endeavors. Making and keeping up with reasonable settling locales is urgent, whether through the insurance of normal environments or the establishment of counterfeit designs like home boxes and mud banks. Preservationists team up with nearby networks, landowners, and legislatures to lay out and keep up with untamed life cordial spaces that take care of the particular requirements of swallow species.

Moderating Environmental Change Effects: A Test of skill and endurance:

As environmental change keeps on modifying worldwide weather conditions, relieving its effects on swallow populaces turns into a test of skill and endurance. Preservation procedures remember checking changes for movement designs, concentrating on the accessibility of bug prey, and executing versatile administration rehearses. Endeavors to decrease by and large fossil fuel byproducts and bring issues to light about environmental change's effect on swallows add to more extensive drives pointed toward safeguarding the natural equilibrium.

Local area Commitment: Encouraging Stewardship and Concurrence:

Connecting with neighborhood networks is crucial to fruitful swallow protection. Training and mindfulness programs cultivate a comprehension of the crucial job swallows play in neighborhood environments and feature the meaning of conjunction. By including networks in home box programs, resident science drives, and natural surroundings rebuilding projects, a feeling of stewardship is developed, making an aggregate liability regarding the prosperity of these avian miracles.

Progressing Logical Exploration: The Way to Informed Preservation:

Logical examination stays at the front of informed protection procedures. Progressing concentrates on swallow conduct, movement designs, regenerative science, and reactions to ecological changes give basic bits of knowledge. Mechanical developments, including GPS following, acoustic checking, and satellite symbolism, engage analysts to accumulate thorough information, upgrading how we might interpret swallow environment and directing designated protection endeavors.

Strategy Promotion: Impacting Change at a Large scale Level:

Support for strategy changes is crucial for address the overall difficulties looked by swallow species. Protection associations, specialists, and energetic people advocate for the consideration of swallow-accommodating practices in metropolitan preparation, maintainable horticulture, and more extensive natural arrangements. By impacting regulation and strategy systems, advocates add to establishing a climate helpful for swallow preservation for a bigger scope.

1. Importance of swallows in ecosystems

In the mind boggling embroidered artwork of Earth's environments, swallows arise as magnetic and naturally huge avian species. Their ethereal tumbling and multifaceted ways of behaving enamor eyewitnesses as well as assume a crucial part in keeping up with the sensitive equilibrium of different biological systems around the world. From bug control to adding to supplement cycles, swallows, having a place with the family Hirundinidae, weave a key string in the texture of biodiversity. In this investigation, we dig into the multi-layered significance of swallows in biological systems, disentangling the perplexing jobs they play and the sweeping effects of their presence on the wellbeing and working of different living spaces.

1. **Bother Control: A Characteristic Avian Partner:**

   One of the essential natural administrations given by swallows lies in their job as capable bug trackers. Swallows are famous for their insatiable hunger for flying bugs, including mosquitoes, flies, moths, and insects. As they smoothly dip and jump through the air, they act as normal nuisance control specialists, assisting with holding bug populaces in line. This nuisance control capability is especially significant in farming scenes, where swallows add to decreasing the requirement for compound pesticides, cultivating a more maintainable and adjusted environment.

2. **Controlling Bug Populaces: Keeping up with Environment Harmony:**

   Swallows effectively take part in managing bug populaces, adding to the harmony of biological systems. By going after bugs that are many times considered farming nuisances, swallows give a characteristic type of vermin the board. This advantages ranchers by lessening crop harm as well as fore-stalls the unrestrained expansion of bug populaces that could upset the more extensive food web. The presence of swallows in different environments goes about as an orchestrating force, adding to the general wellbeing and strength of biological systems.

3. **Supplement Cycling: Swallows as Supporters of Biological system Wellbeing:**

   The job of swallows reaches out past vermin control; they additionally add to supplement cycling in biological systems. Swallow guano, wealthy in nitrogen and other fundamental supplements, fills in as an important manure. The droppings of swallows kept in and around settling destinations add to soil fruitfulness, affecting plant development and generally environment efficiency. This regular treatment process highlights the interconnected connections inside biological systems, showing the way that the exercises of one animal varieties can have flowing consequences for the strength of the whole local area.

4. **Biodiversity Pointers: An Indicator of Environment Wellbeing:**

   Swallows, as delicate and responsive species, go about as important marks of environment wellbeing. Changes in swallow populaces can flag shifts in ecological circumstances, remembering adjustments for bug overflow, environment accessibility, and environment designs. Checking the prosperity of swallow populaces gives experiences into more extensive biological system elements, permitting researchers and traditionalists to evaluate the general wellbeing and strength of environments. Swallows subsequently become living gauges, mirroring the unpredictable snare of life that encompasses them.

5. **Seed Dispersal: An Unheralded Natural Assistance:**

   Certain swallow species, like the Violet-green Swallow (Tachycineta thalassina) and the Tree Swallow (Tachycineta bicolor), assume a part in seed dispersal. As these swallows scavenge on foods grown from the ground, they unintentionally transport seeds to new areas. This cycle adds to the scattering of plant species, cultivating hereditary variety and helping with the colonization of new regions. The apparently basic demonstration of taking care of turns into a significant environmental help, impacting the dissemination and variety of vegetation inside biological systems.

6. **Social Importance: Meshing Swallows into Mankind's Set of experiences:**

Past their biological jobs, swallows hold social importance in mankind's set of experiences, legends, and customs. Their occasional relocations, return to settling destinations, and relationship with specific scenes have motivated fantasies, stories, and creative portrayals across different societies. The social significance of swallows fills in as a sign of the multifaceted association among people and the normal world. This social importance adds to the more extensive comprehension of swallows as fundamental parts of biological systems, in environmental terms as well as inside the texture of human stories.

7. **Fertilization: Swallows as Whimsical Pollinators:**

While swallows are not customary pollinators like honey bees or butterflies, they incidentally add to fertilization. As they visit blossoms looking for nectar, their heads come into contact with conceptive designs, moving dust starting with one sprout then onto the next. This accidental fertilization administration, however not their essential environmental job, grandstands the interconnected connections between various parts of biological systems. Swallows, as they continued looking for food, coincidentally add to the conceptive progress of blooming plants, subsequently upgrading flower variety and supporting other pollinator species.

8. **Keeping up with Amphibian Environments: The Job of Swallows in Riparian Zones:**

Certain swallow species, for example, the Bank Swallow (riparia), are firmly connected with riparian zones and waterways. These regions act as indispensable settling destinations for swallows, giving vertical banks appropriate to their trademark tunnel homes. Swallows in riparian zones add to the wellbeing of amphibian environments by controlling bug populaces, forestalling the excess of sea-going bugs that could adversely affect water quality and the more extensive oceanic food web. Their presence becomes essential to the biological equilibrium of both earthbound and oceanic environments.

9. **Improving Biodiversity Through Settling Destinations:**

The one of a kind settling ways of behaving of swallows, whether building mud homes, using holes, or taking on fake designs, add to living space variety. The accessibility of different settling locales upholds various different species, from bugs and insects that occupy the little hiding spots of homes to other bird species that may entrepreneurially utilize deserted swallow homes. This variety in settling environments upgrades generally biodiversity inside biological systems, cultivating a rich embroidery of life.

10. **Supporting Transitory Network: Rising above Geographic Limits:**

Many swallow species are famous for their amazing transitory excursions, traversing landmasses and associating biological systems across tremendous distances. Their transitory examples add to the idea of transient network, featuring the relationship of territories along their relocation courses. Safeguarding reproducing, visit, and wintering destinations becomes significant to guaranteeing the endurance of transient swallow populaces. Endeavors to monitor these destinations contribute not exclusively to the prosperity of swallows yet in addition to the more extensive protection of transitory bird species and the environments they cross.

B. Overview of the current status of swallow populations

The swallows, with their entrancing ethereal showcases and critical biological jobs, have long held a position of importance in the regular world. In any case, as we explore the intricacies of the advanced period, the prosperity of swallow populaces faces remarkable difficulties. This thorough outline dives into the ongoing status of swallow populaces, investigating the elements affecting their elements, investigating local varieties, and assessing continuous protection endeavors. From populace patterns and dangers to the complexities of checking and research, this assessment tries to give a nuanced comprehension of the current situation with swallow populaces internationally.

1. **Populace Patterns: A Worldwide Point of view:**

   Understanding the ongoing status of swallow populaces requires a worldwide viewpoint, taking into account the different scope of species circulated across mainlands. While some swallow species display steady or expanding populaces, others face declines of fluctuating degrees. Key variables affecting these patterns incorporate environment misfortune, environmental change, pesticide use, and adjustments in bug overflow. Cooperative worldwide endeavors, like the IUCN Red Rundown of Undermined Species, give important bits of knowledge into the protection status of individual swallow species, helping with the appraisal of worldwide populace patterns.

   1.1 Local Varieties:

   Swallow populaces display prominent provincial varieties, affected by neighborhood natural circumstances, land-use practices, and human connections. In North America, for instance, the Stable Swallow (Hirundo rustica) has encountered populace declines, with environment misfortune, agrarian strengthening, and changes in bug overflow adding to this pattern. In Europe, the Normal House Martin (Delichon urbicum) faces difficulties connected with settling site accessibility, exacerbated by changes in building rehearses. Understanding these provincial subtleties is basic for fitting preservation methodologies that address explicit dangers and advance the recuperation of swallow populaces.

2. **Dangers to Swallow Populaces: Disentangling the Perplexing Embroidered artwork:**

Swallows stand up to a heap of dangers that on the whole shape their populace elements. Territory misfortune because of urbanization, horticultural development, and deforestation positions among the essential difficulties. Environmental change presents intricacies, modifying movement designs, impacting bug accessibility, and influencing the planning of rearing seasons. Pesticide use, contamination, and the shortage of appropriate settling destinations further compound the difficulties looked by swallows. Perceiving the interconnected idea of these dangers is significant for carrying out successful preservation estimates that address the complex tensions on swallow populaces.

2.1 Environment Misfortune and Fracture:

As human populaces extend and scenes go through change, swallows wrestle with environment misfortune and fracture. Urbanization, rural escalation, and foundation advancement infringe upon regular settling locales, lessening the accessibility of reasonable natural surroundings. The change of open spaces into metropolitan scenes disturbs the conventional settling destinations of swallows, influencing their regenerative achievement and adding to populace declines.

2.2 Environmental Change Effects:

Environmental change acquaints a unique component with the difficulties looked by swallow populaces. Modifications in temperature, precipitation examples, and occasional prompts impact the accessibility of bugs, an essential food hotspot for swallows. Changes in transient examples, settling ways of behaving, and the synchronicity between hatchling rise and pinnacle bug overflow represent extra difficulties. Adjusting to these environment initiated changes becomes critical for the drawn out endurance of swallow populaces.

2.3 Pesticide Use and Contamination:

The unavoidable utilization of pesticides in rural practices represents an immediate danger to swallow populaces. Insect poisons, planned to control rural irritations, unintentionally influence swallow prey, prompting decreases in bug overflow. Besides, contamination from compound spillover and toxins in water bodies can influence the soundness of swallows and their prey, further fueling populace challenges. Moderating the effect of rural synthetics and tending to water contamination arises as fundamentally important in protecting swallow populaces.

2.4 Settling Site Difficulties:

The accessibility of reasonable settling destinations is a basic element impacting swallow populaces. Changes in building rehearses, the fixing of overhang and cleft, and the evacuation of customary settling structures diminish settling potential open doors for swallows. Fake designs, like scaffolds and structures, can offer option settling locales, yet unsettling influences and annihilation of these destinations represent extra dangers. Preserving and giving proper settling structures becomes indispensable to supporting swallow populaces.

3. **Protection Endeavors: Exploring the Way to Recuperation:**

Perceiving the desperation of tending to the dangers looked by swallow populaces, preservation endeavors have been started around the world. These endeavors include a range of methodologies, from living space reclamation and local area commitment to strategy backing and logical examination. Co-operative undertakings including legislative offices, non-benefit associations, specialists, and nearby networks are fundamental for creating and executing powerful protection measures.

3.1 Environment Rebuilding and Creation:

Reestablishing and making reasonable environments for swallows is a foundation of protection endeavors. This includes safeguarding normal settling locales, for example, vertical banks for tunneling species or mud banks for those developing mud homes. Furthermore, making fake designs, for example, home boxes and edges, gives elective settling open doors in metropolitan and country scenes. Natural surroundings reclamation drives contribute not exclusively to the recuperation of swallow populaces yet in addition to the more extensive upgrade of biodiversity in environments.

3.2 Local area Commitment and Instruction:

Connecting with neighborhood networks is vital for effective swallow preservation. Local area based drives include bringing issues to light about the natural significance of swallows, giving data on home box establishment, and empowering rehearses that help swallow-accommodating conditions. Instructive projects in schools, local area occasions, and resident science projects encourage a feeling of stewardship and aggregate liability, engaging networks to add to effectively swallow preservation.

3.3 Strategy Support: Impacting Preservation for a Bigger Scope:

Support for strategy changes is vital to tending to the all-encompassing difficulties looked by swallow populaces. Protection associations, analysts, and enthusiastic people advocate for the consideration of swallow-accommodating practices in metropolitan preparation, supportable agribusiness, and more extensive natural arrangements. By impacting regulation and strategy systems, advocates add to establishing a climate helpful for swallow preservation for a bigger scope.

3.4 Logical Exploration and Checking:

Logical examination assumes a vital part in grasping the elements of swallow populaces and illuminating designated protection systems. Continuous examination drives center around observing populace patterns, concentrating on reproducing ways of behaving, and researching the effects of natural elements. Innovative headways, for example, GPS following, acoustic checking, and satellite symbolism, improve information assortment and examination, giving important experiences to confirm based preservation endeavors.

3.5 Worldwide Cooperation: A Worldwide Way to deal with Preservation:

Given the transitory idea of many swallow species, global coordinated effort is fundamental for their protection. Joint examination drives, transboundary protection arrangements, and the trading of best practices add to an all encompassing comprehension of swallow populaces. Cooperative endeavors include sharing information on movement courses, planning protection measures across lines, and cultivating a worldwide local area devoted to the prosperity of swallows.

4. **Observing and Exploration: Enlightening the Way ahead:**

An exhaustive comprehension of the ebb and flow status of swallow populaces depends on hearty observing and research drives. Constant endeavors to follow populace patterns, study settling ways of behaving, and evaluate the effects of natural changes give the establishment to informed protection procedures. Long haul checking programs, resident science projects, and mechanical developments add to the aggregation of information fundamental for adjusting protection endeavors to advancing conditions.

4.1 Resident Science Drives: Drawing in General society in Protection:

Connecting with general society in logical undertakings through resident science drives is a useful asset for swallow observing. Resident researchers add to information assortment, including perceptions of settling ways of behaving, movement examples, and populace elements. This cooperative methodology improves the amount of accessible information as well as cultivates a feeling of association and divided liability between the more extensive local area.

4.2 Constant Checking Advancements: Bridling Development for Preservation:

Mechanical developments continuously observing proposition uncommon bits of knowledge into the existences of swallows. GPS beacons, radio telemetry, and acoustic observing frameworks empower scientists to follow individual birds, screen movement courses, and study vocalizations. These innovations give a unique comprehension of swallow conduct, taking into consideration versatile protection systems in light of continuous information.

4.3 Long haul Observing Projects: Graphing Patterns Over the long run:

Laying out long haul observing projects is fundamental for exhaustively surveying the situation with swallow populaces. These projects include efficient information assortment overstretched periods, empowering the distinguishing proof of patterns, changes, and likely dangers. Long haul checking adds to the distinguishing proof of key rearing destinations, basic transient courses, and regions requiring designated preservation intercessions.

C. Purpose of the book: raising awareness and proposing conservation strategies

Notwithstanding heightening dangers to swallow populaces around the world, the requirement for far reaching mindfulness and compelling preservation methodologies has never been more pressing. "Wings of Progress," the reason driven book at the core of this story, leaves determined to enlighten the situation of swallows, explain the mind boggling trap of difficulties they face, and propose substantial protection methodologies pointed toward getting their future. This investigation dives into the overall motivation behind the book — bringing issues to light and pushing for noteworthy preservation estimates that rise above geographic limits, rousing an aggregate obligation to shielding these ethereal wonders.

1. Grasping the Goal: The Territory of Swallow Populaces:

The book's establishment lies in giving an exhaustive comprehension of the present status of swallow populaces. It enlightens the multi-layered difficulties, territorial varieties, and worldwide patterns impacting the prosperity of these avian miracles. Through connecting with stories, upheld by logical bits of knowledge and true models, perusers are drenched in the realm of swallows, acquiring a significant appreciation for their natural importance, social significance, and the dangers that endanger their reality.

1.1 Revealing Dangers to Swallow Populaces:

The book fastidiously unwinds the mind boggling embroidered artwork of dangers confronting swallow populaces, going from territory misfortune and environmental change to pesticide use and settling site difficulties. By giving a complete outline of these difficulties, the story looks to highlight the direness of activity and the interconnected idea of the issues that effect swallow populaces on a worldwide scale.

1.2 Local Subtleties and Worldwide Viewpoints:

Understanding the local subtleties of swallow populaces is central to figuring out viable protection techniques. "Wings of Progress" takes perusers on an excursion across landmasses, investigating the different difficulties looked by swallow species in various districts. This worldwide viewpoint not just widens the peruser's perception of the difficulties yet in addition underscores the requirement for cooperative, transboundary protection endeavors that rise above international limits.

2. **Bringing issues to light: Making a Convincing Story:**

At the core of the book's motivation is the undertaking to bring issues to light, winding around a convincing story that enraptures perusers and rouses a feeling of association with the normal world. Through distinctive narrating, logical bits of knowledge, and tales, the book means to rise above customary preservation talk, drawing in perusers sincerely and mentally.

2.1 Winding around the Narrative of Swallows:

"Wings of Progress" places swallows at the focal point of the story, changing them from simple subjects of study to charming heroes in an account of endurance. By diving into the complexities of swallow conduct, movement, and settling, the book makes a close to home association that rises above scholastic talk. Through narrating, the story looks to cultivate compassion and a profound appreciation for the existences of these avian miracles.

2.2 Developing a Feeling of Stewardship:

The book goes past simple mindfulness, intending to develop a feeling of stewardship among its perusers. By explaining the basic environmental jobs that swallows play, the story welcomes perusers to consider their individual and aggregate liability in safeguarding these fundamental bird species. This shift from detached attention to dynamic stewardship shapes the foundation of the book's motivation, empowering perusers to become advocates for swallow protection.

3. **Protection Techniques: From Attention to Activity:**

While mindfulness is an essential initial step, "Wings of Progress" goes further by proposing a range of protection techniques. These systems are educated by logical examination as well as intended to be useful, versatile, and adaptable, guaranteeing their importance across different scenes and settings.

3.1 Territory Protection and Rebuilding:

A focal fundamental of the proposed protection systems is natural surroundings conservation and reclamation. The book advocates for the assurance of normal settling locales, the production of fake designs, and the rebuilding of natural surroundings helpful for swallow populaces. By illustrating explicit activities, for example, the establishment of home boxes and the safeguarding of open spaces, the story enables perusers to add to territory protection in their neighborhood surroundings effectively.

3.2 Environmental Change Moderation and Transformation:

Perceiving the effect of environmental change on swallow populaces, the book dives into methodologies for alleviation and transformation. From upholding for more extensive drives to decrease fossil fuel byproducts to advancing nearby measures that help swallows despite changing climatic circumstances, the proposed techniques plan to address the all-encompassing test of environmental change with down to earth and reachable activities.

3.3 Local area Commitment and Resident Science:

The book highlights the essential job of networks in swallow preservation. It proposes systems for local area commitment, from instructive projects in schools to cooperative drives that include nearby occupants in checking and protection endeavors. The advancement of resident science projects arises as a useful asset, transforming nearby networks into dynamic supporters of logical information and information assortment.

3.4 Strategy Promotion and Institutional Help:

Perceiving the requirement for foundational change, "Wings of Progress" advocates for strategy changes and institutional help. The story underscores the significance of coordinating swallow-accommodating practices into metropolitan preparation, agrarian strategies, and ecological guidelines. By illustrating the expected effect of strategy backing, the book tries to rouse perusers to draw in with chiefs and add to the detailing of preservation cordial approaches.

3.5 Global Cooperation: A Brought together Front for Preservation:

The book support the possibility of worldwide coordinated effort as a fundamental component in swallow preservation. It features effective contextual investigations of cross-line drives, energizes the trading of best practices, and requires a brought together worldwide exertion. By exhibiting the interconnected idea of swallow relocation courses and natural surroundings, the story supports that compelling preservation requires a cooperative and facilitated approach.

4. Logical Exploration and Checking: Building Information for Activity:

A basic part of the proposed preservation procedures includes continuous logical examination and observing. "Wings of Progress" focuses on the significance of constant review to adjust procedures in view of advancing conditions. By cultivating a culture of interest and request, the book urges perusers to help and draw in with logical examination drives, adding to the information base fundamental for powerful protection.

4.1 Long haul Observing Projects: Supporting Protection Endeavors:

The book advocates for the foundation of long haul observing projects to follow swallow populaces overstretched periods. These projects give fundamental information to surveying patterns, recognizing arising dangers, and assessing the viability of preservation measures. By stressing the significance of supported checking, the story highlights the requirement for a guarantee to long haul preservation endeavors.

4.2 Using Innovation for Continuous Checking: Development for Protection:

Mechanical developments, for example, GPS following, acoustic observing, and ongoing information assortment, assume a vital part in present day protection endeavors. "Wings of Progress" investigates the capability of these advances in improving checking capacities, giving continuous experiences into swallow conduct, relocation examples, and reactions to natural changes. By demystifying innovation, the story looks to motivate perusers to embrace imaginative methodologies in the assistance of protection.

Chapter 1

Swallow Species Overview

Swallows, individuals from the Hirundinidae family, incorporate a different gathering of passerine birds known for their coordinated flight and gymnastic moves. This outline gives a top to bottom investigation of different swallow species, revealing insight into their exceptional qualities, territories, and movement designs.

The Intriguing Universe of Swallows

Swallows are circulated internationally, possessing different environments, from open fields and prairies to wetlands and metropolitan regions. Their unmistakable pointed wings, forked tails, and smooth bodies are all around adjusted for fast and nimble flight, making them dazzling subjects for bird devotees and specialists the same.

1. **Horse shelter Swallow (Hirundo rustica)**

   The Animal dwellingplace Swallow, with its striking cobalt-blue upperparts and cinnamon-shaded underparts, is one of the most broadly perceived swallow species. Known for its relationship with human designs, the Outbuilding Swallow assembles cup-molded homes in stables, sheds, and other man-made structures. This species embraces exceptional significant distance movements, covering large number of kilometers among reproducing and wintering grounds.

2. **Precipice Swallow (Petrochelidon pyrrhonota)**

   Recognized by its square-tipped tail and unmistakably hued temple, the Precipice Swallow is a pilgrim nester that forms gourd-molded settles commonly tracked down on bluffs, extensions, or structures. These common settling propensities give security against hunters as well as cultivate social cooperations among settlement individuals. The Precipice Swallow's transient conduct takes it from North America to South America, navigating great distances.

3. **Tree Swallow (Tachycineta bicolor)**

Exquisitely embellished in luminous blue and white plumage, the Tree Swallow is known for its pit settling propensities. It chooses tree depressions, home boxes, or even deserted woodpecker openings for reproducing. Dissimilar to some other swallow species, Tree Swallows are hole settling subject matter experts, depending on existing designs instead of developing elaborate homes. Their rearing reach traverses North America, and their transient processes take them toward the southern US and Mexico.

4. **Welcome Swallow (Hirundo neoxena)**

Endemic to Australasia, the Welcome Swallow is described by its steel-blue upperparts and particularly lengthy, profoundly forked tail. Frequently found close to water bodies, these swallows participate in gymnastic trips over open regions, getting bugs on the wing. Their cup-molded homes, built with mud pellets, are commonly joined to man-made designs, precipices, or other reasonable surfaces.

5. **Wire-followed Swallow (Hirundo smithii)**

Living in sub-Saharan Africa and portions of the Center East, the Wire-followed Swallow stands apart because of its astoundingly long tail decorations. These decorations, frequently surpassing the length of the bird's body, add to its smooth appearance during flight. The Wire-followed Swallow chooses open territories close to water bodies for rearing, developing cup-molded homes on level branches or bluffs.

6. **Bank Swallow (riparia)**

Named for its inclination for settling in earthen banks or precipices, the Bank Swallow is a transitory animal types tracked down across the Northern Half of the globe. Unmistakable by its brown and white plumage, the Bank Swallow makes tunnels in sandy or loamy soils for settling. These settlements frequently number in the hundreds, displaying their social and public settling conduct.

7. **Red-rumped Swallow (Cecropis daurica)**

Endemic to Europe, Asia, and portions of Africa, the Red-rumped Swallow is known for its energetic plumage, including a cinnamon-hued posterior and blue upperparts. Favoring open nation environments, this species develops cup-molded homes on edges or underneath overhangs. Their broad transient excursions take them from favorable places in Europe to wintering regions in Africa and Asia.

8. **Purple Martin (Progne subis)**

The biggest swallow species in North America, the Purple Martin flaunts a striking purple-blue plumage. Not at all like different swallows, Purple Martins are pit settling experts that depend on man-made structures, for example, extraordinarily planned martin houses, for rearing. These birds are exceptionally friendly, frequently framing enormous states during the reproducing season, and their transitory examples cover huge distances, from North to South America.

9. **Pacific Swallow (Hirundo tahitica)**

Local to Southeast Asia and the Pacific Islands, the Pacific Swallow grandstands a special blend of metallic blue upperparts and an unmistakable chestnut-shaded throat. Flourishing in different environments, from seaside regions to backwoods, this swallow species builds cup-molded homes on level branches. Its transitory conduct shifts, for certain populaces being occupant, while others embrace occasional developments.

10. **American Precipice Swallow (Petrochelidon pyrrhonota)**

Comparative in appearance to the Precipice Swallow, the American Bluff Swallow is tracked down across North America. Conspicuous by its square-tipped tail and rufous brow, this species takes part in pioneer settling, frequently picking structures like extensions or bluffs. Their exceptional transitory excursions take them from North America to Focal and South America, displaying the tremendous distances covered during relocation.

1.1Introduction to different swallow species

Swallows, individuals from the Hirundinidae family, enthrall bird devotees and analysts the same with their elegant flight, gymnastic moves, and lively plumage. This presentation digs into the assorted universe of swallow species, unwinding the exceptional attributes, living spaces, and relocation designs that characterize every individual from this avian family.

1. **The Animal dwellingplace Swallow (Hirundo rustica)**

The notorious Horse shelter Swallow stands apart with its cobalt-blue upperparts, cinnamon-shaded underparts, and profoundly forked tail. A worldwide conveyed animal types, the Horse shelter Swallow has a nearby relationship with human designs, frequently fabricating cup-formed homes in outbuildings, sheds, and other man-made conditions. Its transient ability is exceptional, covering large number of kilometers among rearing and wintering grounds. The Animal dwellingplace Swallow's versatility to human-modified scenes has added to its inescapable presence on pretty much every landmass.

2. **The Bluff Swallow (Petrochelidon pyrrhonota)**

Recognized by a square-tipped tail and a particularly shaded brow, the Precipice Swallow is known for its frontier settling propensities. This species develops gourd-formed settles regularly tracked down on bluffs, extensions, or even structures. Settlements of Precipice Swallows give insurance against hunters as well as cultivate social cooperations among state individuals. Their transient process from North America to South America is a demonstration of their perseverance and navigational abilities, covering tremendous distances across different scenes.

3. **The Tree Swallow (Tachycineta bicolor)**

Decorated in radiant blue and white plumage, the Tree Swallow is a pit settling trained professional. It chooses tree pits, home boxes, or even deserted woodpecker openings for rearing. Dissimilar to some other swallow species, Tree Swallows depend on existing designs instead of building elaborate homes. Their reproducing range traverses North America, and their transient processes take them toward the southern US and Mexico. The Tree Swallow's inclination for open natural surroundings close to water grandstands its versatility to different environments.

4. **The Welcome Swallow (Hirundo neoxena)**

Endemic to Australasia, the Welcome Swallow is portrayed by steel-blue upperparts and a particularly lengthy, profoundly forked tail. Frequently found close to water bodies, these swallows participate in aerobatic trips over open regions, getting bugs on the wing. Their cup-formed homes, developed with mud pellets, are regularly joined to man-made designs, precipices, or other appropriate surfaces. The Welcome Swallow's presence in metropolitan and provincial conditions underscores its capacity to flourish across assorted scenes.

5. **The Wire-followed Swallow (Hirundo smithii)**

Dwelling in sub-Saharan Africa and portions of the Center East, the Wire-followed Swallow stands apart because of its astoundingly long tail decorations. These decorations, frequently surpassing the length of the bird's body, add to its elegant appearance during flight. The Wire-followed Swallow chooses open territories close to water bodies for reproducing, building cup-molded homes on flat branches or bluffs. Its striking appearance and novel settling conduct make it an enthralling subject for birdwatchers and specialists the same.

6. **The Bank Swallow (riparia)**

Named for its inclination for settling in earthen banks or bluffs, the Bank Swallow is a transitory animal groups tracked down across the Northern Half of the globe. Unmistakable by its brown and white plumage, the Bank Swallow makes tunnels in sandy or loamy soils for settling. These states frequently number in the hundreds, displaying their social and public settling conduct. The Bank Swallow's transitory excursion, set apart by aggregate takeoffs and appearances, highlights the coordination inside these avian networks.

7. **The Red-rumped Swallow (Cecropis daurica)**

Endemic to Europe, Asia, and portions of Africa, the Red-rumped Swallow is known for its lively plumage, including a cinnamon-hued rear end and blue upperparts. Inclining toward open nation environments, this species develops cup-formed homes on edges or underneath overhangs. Their broad transitory excursions take them from favorable places in Europe to wintering regions in Africa and Asia. The Red-rumped Swallow's versatility to different biological systems makes it an intriguing subject for natural examinations.

8. **The Purple Martin (Progne subis)**

The biggest swallow species in North America, the Purple Martin flaunts striking purple-blue plumage. Dissimilar to different swallows, Purple Martins are pit settling experts that depend on man-made structures, for example, uniquely planned martin houses, for rearing. Profoundly friendly, they frequently structure huge settlements during the rearing season. Their transient examples cover immense distances, from North to South America, displaying the amazing accomplishments of perseverance during their occasional developments.

9. **The Pacific Swallow (Hirundo tahitica)**

Local to Southeast Asia and the Pacific Islands, the Pacific Swallow features a special mix of metallic blue upperparts and an unmistakable chestnut-hued throat. Flourishing in various living spaces, from beach front regions to woodlands, this swallow species develops cup-formed homes on even branches. While certain populaces are occupant, others attempt occasional developments, mirroring their flexibility to changing biological circumstances.

10. **The American Precipice Swallow (Petrochelidon pyrrhonota)**

Comparable in appearance to the Precipice Swallow, the American Bluff Swallow is tracked down across North America. Unmistakable by its square-tipped tail and rufous temple, this species takes part in pioneer settling, frequently picking structures like extensions or precipices. Their noteworthy transient excursions take them from North America to Focal and South America, exhibiting the huge distances covered during movement. The American Precipice Swallow's presence in different living spaces highlights its versatility across environments.

1.2Unique characteristics and habitats of each species

The Horse shelter Swallow is a particular animal categories known for its striking cobalt-blue upperparts and cinnamon-shaded underparts. One of its novel qualities is the profoundly forked tail, an element that separates it from other swallow species. Animal dwellingplace Swallows are exceptionally versatile and are many times tracked down in close relationship with human designs. Their cup-formed homes, developed with mud pellets, are normally inherent stables, sheds, or other man-made conditions. They have a surprising worldwide dissemination and embrace broad relocations, covering great many kilometers among reproducing and wintering grounds.

Precipice Swallow (Petrochelidon pyrrhonota):

The Precipice Swallow is described by a square-tipped tail and an unmistakably hued brow. One of its extraordinary highlights is its pilgrim settling conduct. These swallows develop gourd-molded settles regularly tracked down on precipices, scaffolds, or even structures. The states, frequently involving many people, give insurance against hunters as well as encourage social collaborations among settlement individuals. Precipice Swallows display amazing transitory excursions from North America to South America, exhibiting their perseverance and navigational abilities.

Tree Swallow (Tachycineta bicolor):

The Tree Swallow stands apart with its glowing blue and white plumage. Not at all like some other swallow species, Tree Swallows are depression settling trained professionals. They select tree depressions, home boxes, or even deserted woodpecker openings for rearing. This remarkable settling conduct recognizes them from different species in the family. Their transitory excursions take them from their favorable places in North America toward the southern US and Mexico. The flexibility of Tree Swallows to different environments, from open fields to wetlands, features their adaptability.

Welcome Swallow (Hirundo neoxena):

The Welcome Swallow, endemic to Australasia, is described by steel-blue upperparts and a particularly lengthy, profoundly forked tail. This species is much of the time found close to water bodies, taking part in aerobatic trips over open regions to get bugs on the wing. Their cup-molded homes, developed with mud pellets, are commonly joined to man-made designs, precipices, or other appropriate surfaces. The Welcome Swallow's capacity to flourish in metropolitan and rustic conditions features its versatility to different scenes.

Wire-followed Swallow (Hirundo smithii):

Living in sub-Saharan Africa and portions of the Center East, the Wire-followed Swallow is known for its astoundingly long tail decorations. These decorations, frequently surpassing the length of the bird's body, add to its agile appearance during flight. The Wire-followed Swallow chooses open living spaces close to water bodies for reproducing, building cup-molded homes on level branches or bluffs. Its interesting tail decorations and settling conduct make it a dazzling subject for birdwatchers and specialists.

Bank Swallow (riparia):

Named for its inclination for settling in earthen banks or precipices, the Bank Swallow is a transitory animal categories tracked down across the Northern Half of the globe. Conspicuous by its brown and white plumage, the Bank Swallow makes tunnels in sandy or loamy soils for settling. These provinces frequently number in the hundreds, exhibiting their social and shared settling conduct. The Bank Swallow's transitory excursion, set apart by aggregate flights and appearances, highlights the coordination inside these avian networks.

Red-rumped Swallow (Cecropis daurica):

Endemic to Europe, Asia, and portions of Africa, the Red-rumped Swallow is known for its dynamic plumage, highlighting a cinnamon-shaded posterior and blue upperparts. Inclining toward open nation living spaces, this species builds cup-molded homes on edges or underneath overhangs. Their broad transitory excursions take them from favorable places in Europe to wintering regions in Africa and Asia. The Red-rumped Swallow's flexibility to different biological systems makes it an interesting subject for environmental investigations.

Purple Martin (Progne subis):

The Purple Martin, the biggest swallow species in North America, flaunts striking purple-blue plumage. Dissimilar to different swallows, Purple Martins are hole settling subject matter experts, depending on man-made designs, for example, extraordinarily planned martin houses for reproducing. Profoundly friendly, they frequently structure enormous provinces during the rearing season. Their transient examples cover huge distances, from North to South America, displaying the wonderful accomplishments of perseverance during their occasional developments.

Pacific Swallow (Hirundo tahitica):

Local to Southeast Asia and the Pacific Islands, the Pacific Swallow exhibits an exceptional blend of metallic blue upperparts and a particular chestnut-hued throat. Flourishing in different living spaces, from seaside regions to woodlands, this swallow species develops cup-formed homes on even branches. While certain populaces are inhabitant, others attempt occasional developments, mirroring their versatility to changing natural circumstances.

American Precipice Swallow (Petrochelidon pyrrhonota):

Comparative in appearance to the Precipice Swallow, the American Bluff Swallow is tracked down across North America. Conspicuous by its square-tipped tail and rufous temple, this species participates in pioneer settling, frequently picking structures like extensions or precipices. Their wonderful transient excursions take them from North America to Focal and South America, displaying the huge distances covered during movement. The American Bluff Swallow's presence in different living spaces highlights its versatility across environments.

1.3 Distribution and migration patterns

The investigation of dissemination and relocation designs is a complex investigation that dives into the development and scattering of different components inside the normal and human domains. Whether looking at the circulation of species in environments or the relocation examples of human populaces, these peculiarities assume a pivotal part in molding the elements of our reality. This article means to give a far reaching outline of conveyance and movement designs, investigating their importance, causes, and suggestions across various spaces.

1. **Dissemination Examples in Nature:**

   Environmental Dissemination:

Natural circulation alludes to the game plan and wealth of species in various environments. It is impacted by a horde of variables, including environment, geography, and communications between species. One outstanding model is the zonation of vegetation in uneven locales, where particular plant networks are circulated in view of elevation. Understanding environmental conveyance designs is fundamental for protection endeavors, as it supports recognizing key natural surroundings and weak species.

Biodiversity Areas of interest:

Biodiversity areas of interest are regions with outstandingly elevated degrees of species wealth and endemism. These districts, like the Amazon Rainforest and the Coral Triangle, are basic for worldwide biodiversity. Examining dispersion designs inside these areas of interest assists analysts with pinpointing areas of preservation need. Factors, for example, environment dependability and land history add to the arrangement of biodiversity areas of interest.

Maritime Conveyance:

Marine environments show remarkable appropriation designs impacted by sea flows, temperature angles, and supplement accessibility. The relocation of marine species, like whales and fish, is frequently attached to these examples. Understanding maritime appropriation is pivotal for supportable fisheries the board and the preservation of marine biodiversity.

2. **Movement Examples in Nature:**

Creature Relocation:

Creature relocation is an interesting peculiarity seen across different taxa. Birds, warm blooded animals, fish, and even bugs attempt long excursions for rearing, taking care of, or getting away from brutal natural circumstances. The Icy tern, for example, moves large number of miles every year between its favorable places in the Icy and wintering grounds in the Antarctic. Relocation procedures are different and can include route by divine signs, attractive fields, or learned courses.

Bug Relocation:

Bugs, frequently ignored in relocation conversations, assume a significant part in environments. Ruler butterflies, for example, embrace a wonderful multi-generational relocation, crossing large number of miles between their favorable places in North America and wintering locales in Mexico. Understanding bug relocation is fundamental for bug the board, fertilization elements, and environment working.

3. **Human Movement Examples:**

Authentic Human Relocations:

Human movement has been a steady from the beginning of time, molded by different factors like ecological changes, clashes, and financial open doors. The Incomparable Human Movement out of Africa, the colonization of the

Americas, and the Silk Street shipping lanes are authentic models that have essentially affected the appropriation of populaces and societies around the world.

Contemporary Relocation Patterns:

In the cutting edge time, globalization, monetary abberations, and political precariousness keep on driving human movement. The examples change from country to-metropolitan relocation inside nations to worldwide movement streams. Understanding contemporary relocation is significant for resolving issues like outcast emergencies, work portability, and the social variety of metropolitan focuses.

4. **Causes and Systems of Circulation and Movement:**

Ecological Elements:

Natural elements, like environment, geology, and territory accessibility, assume a crucial part in forming conveyance and relocation designs. Species are frequently adjusted to explicit ecological circumstances, impacting where they can flourish and relocate. Changes in environment can prompt changes in appropriation ranges, influencing biological systems all around the world.

Anthropogenic Impacts:

Human exercises, including deforestation, urbanization, and environmental change, significantly affect dissemination and movement designs. These anthropogenic impacts can upset regular living spaces, adjust relocation courses, and lead to the decay of specific species. Protection endeavors should address these human-initiated difficulties to shield biodiversity.

Social and Social Variables:

In human relocation, social and social variables, like language, religion, and financial open doors, frequently assume a critical part. Diasporas and social trades add to the rich woven artwork of human social orders. Understanding these elements is fundamental for cultivating social attachment and addressing difficulties connected with reconciliation and multiculturalism.

5. **Mechanical Advances in Concentrating on Circulation and Relocation:**

Remote Detecting and GIS:

Remote detecting advancements and Geographic Data Frameworks (GIS) have altered the investigation of circulation designs. Satellite symbolism permits scientists to screen changes in land cover, track natural life movements, and survey the effect of human exercises on environments. GIS works with the combination of spatial information, empowering exhaustive examinations of circulation elements.

Following Advances:

Progresses in following advancements, like GPS and satellite labels, have altogether upgraded how we might interpret creature relocation. Specialists can follow the developments of individual creatures progressively, uncovering nitty gritty movement courses and ways of behaving. This data is important for preservation endeavors and the improvement of successful administration methodologies.

6. **Preservation Suggestions:**

Biodiversity Preservation:

Understanding conveyance designs is essential for powerful biodiversity protection. Preservation methodologies can be customized in light of the particular requirements of various species and environments. Safeguarded regions and passageways can be laid out to protect basic environments and work with the development of species.

Environmental Change Variation:

As environmental change modifies conveyance designs, preservation endeavors should adjust to safeguard weak species. Traditionalists can utilize prescient models to expect shifts in appropriation ranges and execute proactive measures to moderate the effect of environmental change on biodiversity.

Maintainable Asset The board:

In both earthbound and marine biological systems, information on dissemination and relocation designs is fundamental for supportable asset the executives. Fisheries can be overseen all the more successfully by grasping the transitory courses of fish species, and land-use arranging can profit from experiences into the dissemination of key plant and creature species.

Chapter 2

Threats To Swallow Populations

Swallows, known for their ethereal tumbling and effortless flight, are a different gathering of birds having a place with the family Hirundinidae. With north of 80 species appropriated around the world, swallows are a vital piece of biological systems, adding to bug control and filling in as marks of natural wellbeing. In any case, in spite of their versatility, swallow populaces face a variety of dangers that have critical ramifications for their endurance. This article plans to give an inside and out investigation of the different dangers influencing swallow populaces, going from natural surroundings misfortune and environmental change to pesticide openness and counterfeit designs.

1. **Environment Misfortune and Debasement:**
   Urbanization and Settling Destinations:
   Swallows, especially those that home in pits or construct mud homes, face difficulties because of urbanization. The change of normal scenes into metropolitan regions frequently brings about the obliteration of appropriate settling destinations. Furthermore, the expansion in cleared surfaces diminishes the accessibility of mud for building homes, affecting species like the Stable Swallow and Bluff Swallow.
   Rural Strengthening:
   Rural practices add to living space misfortune for swallows. The change of different scenes into monoculture fields decreases the overflow of bugs - an essential food hotspot for swallows. Pesticide use in horticulture further mixtures the issue by straightforwardly influencing swallow populaces and draining their prey base.
2. **Environmental Change and Adjusted Movement Examples:**
   Changes in Atmospheric conditions:
   Environmental change has prompted shifts in atmospheric conditions,

influencing the accessibility of food assets for swallows. Changes in precipitation and temperature can affect the planning of bug development, possibly prompting confounds between top food accessibility and swallow rearing seasons.

Modified Movement Courses:

Swallows are known for their momentous significant distance movements. Notwithstanding, environmental change can adjust the timing and courses of these relocations. Changes in temperature and wind examples might influence the overflow and dispersion of bugs along relocation courses, affecting the progress of these excursions.

3. **Pesticide Openness and Contamination:**

Insect poisons and Declining Bug Populaces:

Swallows depend vigorously on bugs for food, and the utilization of bug sprays represents an immediate danger to their food supply. Bug sprays, for example, neonicotinoids, can prompt decreases in bug populaces, influencing the accessibility of prey for swallows. This affects swallow conceptive achievement and by and large populace wellbeing.

Mercury and Weighty Metal Defilement:

Swallows, being insectivores, can amass weighty metals like mercury through their eating regimen. Wetland living spaces, frequently visited by swallows, might be debased with weighty metals from modern spillover. Constant openness to these contaminations can bring about regenerative issues, influencing the suitability of swallow populaces.

4. **Fake Designs and Impacts:**

Crashes with Structures:

The expansion of tall structures represents a critical danger to swallows. Impacts with glass windows and walls are a significant reason for mortality among swallows, especially during their quick and coordinated flights. Measures, for example, window decals and bird-accommodating engineering are fundamental to relieve this danger.

Home Obliteration from Foundation Advancement:

Foundation advancement, including street development and redesign projects, can prompt the annihilation of swallow homes. Swallows frequently construct homes in protected areas, for example, scaffolds and bridges, making them helpless against aggravations brought about by human exercises.

5. **Intrusive Species and Home Contest:**

Rivalry with House Sparrows:

In certain districts, the presentation of obtrusive species, especially the House Sparrow, has prompted expanded contest for settling locales. House Sparrows may forcefully assume control over swallow homes, decreasing the accessibility of reasonable rearing areas for local swallow species.

Predation by Presented Species:

The presentation of non-local hunters, like rodents and felines, can represent a danger to swallow populaces. Homes on the ground or in weak areas become helpless to predation, affecting both grown-up swallows and their posterity.

6. **Infection and Parasites:**

Avian Infections:

Swallow populaces are not resistant to avian illnesses, some of which can prompt huge downfalls. Avian flu and West Nile infection are instances of sicknesses that can influence swallows, affecting their wellbeing and conceptive achievement.

Parasites Affecting Regenerative Achievement:

Swallows might confront difficulties from different parasites, including vermin and insects. Home parasites can adversely influence regenerative accomplishment by influencing the soundness of little birds or diminishing the quantity of eggs laid by grown-up swallows.

7. **Protection Endeavors and Arrangements:**

Environment Protection and Rebuilding:

Safeguarding and reestablishing normal territories is urgent for the preservation of swallow populaces. Endeavors ought to zero in on protecting regions with reasonable settling destinations, including wetlands, open fields, and normal pits. Metropolitan arranging ought to integrate green spaces to keep up with biodiversity.

Protection of Movement Passageways:

Perceiving the significance of movement passages is fundamental for defending swallow populaces. Preservation drives ought to plan to safeguard these courses, guaranteeing that swallows can embrace their relocations without experiencing huge hindrances.

Decreasing Pesticide Use and Advancing Supportable Horticulture:

Carrying out supportable agrarian practices, like coordinated bother the board, can assist with decreasing the dependence on destructive pesticides. Ranchers and policymakers ought to cooperate to advance harmless to the ecosystem cultivating strategies that benefit both horticulture and natural life.

Alleviating Crashes with Structures:

Planning and retrofitting structures to lessen bird impacts is essential for safeguarding swallows and other avian species. The consolidation of bird-accommodating engineering, including designed glass and outer markers, can fundamentally decrease the gamble of crashes.

Obtrusive Species The board:

Controlling and overseeing obtrusive species, especially those that contend with swallows for settling locales, is fundamental. This might include designated control measures for obtrusive species or the reclamation of normal living spaces that help local untamed life.

Checking and Exploration:

Consistent checking and research are basic for figuring out the continuous dangers to swallow populaces. Long haul studies can give bits of knowledge into populace elements, relocation designs, and the viability of protection measures, directing informed navigation.

2.1 Loss of nesting sites due to urbanization and habitat destruction

As urbanization and natural surroundings annihilation keep on reshaping scenes across the globe, quite possibly of the most squeezing challenge looked by avian populaces is the deficiency of settling locales. Metropolitan extension, foundation advancement, and modifications to regular territories have prompted the debasement and fracture of conditions basic for bird settling. This article investigates the multi-layered effect of urbanization and living space annihilation on avian settling destinations, featuring the ramifications for bird species and accentuating the requirement for preservation endeavors to moderate these dangers.

1. **Urbanization: Changing Scenes and Settling Difficulties:**
   Change of Normal Environments:

   Urbanization includes the change of regular scenes into metropolitan regions, prompting the deficiency of urgent settling locales for different bird species. Woodlands, wetlands, and open spaces are frequently supplanted by structures, streets, and other foundation, passing on birds with less reasonable areas to construct homes and back their young.

   Changed Living space Construction:

   The design of metropolitan conditions varies altogether from normal territories, influencing the accessibility of appropriate settling destinations. Many bird species are adjusted to explicit highlights, like trees, bluffs, or thick vegetation, for settling. Metropolitan regions frequently miss the mark on components, compelling birds to adjust to less than ideal circumstances or go after restricted settling spaces.

2. **Environment Annihilation and Fracture:**
   Discontinuity's Effect on Reproducing Achievement:

   Territory annihilation and fracture add to the separation of staying normal regions. This fracture can prompt expanded contest for assets and breaking point the network of natural surroundings fundamental for reproducing. Birds subject to explicit biological systems find it trying to find appropriate settling locales, influencing their rearing achievement and generally speaking populace wellbeing.

Loss of Variety in Settling Choices:

Various biological systems offer a scope of settling choices for various bird species, considering concurrence and diminished contest. Territory obliteration, be that as it may, kills this variety, leaving birds with less decisions. This absence of choices can prompt expanded contest and clashes among bird species, further stressing their capacity to find reasonable settling destinations.

3. **Influence on Unambiguous Bird Species:**

Metropolitan Settling Birds:

Some bird species have adjusted to metropolitan conditions and even flourish in urban communities. Nonetheless, this variation isn't all inclusive, numerous species actually depend on regular environments for settling. Urbanization, consequently, represents a danger to those animal groups incapable to conform to the difficulties of city life.

Raptors and Huge Homes:

Bigger birds, including raptors, frequently require significant settling locales like tall trees or bluffs. As urbanization diminishes the accessibility of these locales, raptors might confront difficulties in tracking down reasonable areas for settling. This can have flowing impacts on the natural pecking order, as raptors assume a critical part in controlling rat populaces.

4. **Protection Difficulties and Arrangements:**

Safeguarding Green Spaces:

The safeguarding of green spaces inside metropolitan regions is fundamental for keeping up with settling locales. Stops, cultivates, and assigned normal regions can act as pivotal shelters for birds, giving fundamental settling choices and adding to metropolitan biodiversity.

Metropolitan Anticipating Bird-Accommodating Urban areas:

Incorporating bird-accommodating plan standards into metropolitan arranging can alleviate the effect of urbanization on settling locales. This incorporates integrating green rooftops, bird-accommodating glass, and keeping a blend of vegetation to make different territories inside cityscapes.

Making Settling Designs:

Executing counterfeit settling structures, like bird enclosures and settling stages, can help make up for the deficiency of normal settling locales. These designs ought to copy the circumstances liked by unambiguous bird species, offering options in metropolitan conditions.

Instructing The general population:

Public mindfulness and schooling programs are fundamental in encouraging a feeling of obligation for metropolitan biodiversity. Empowering occupants to make bird-accommodating spaces in their yards, stay away from aggravation to settling birds, and take part in local area protection drives can add to saving settling destinations.

Reclamation Undertakings:

Environment reclamation projects in corrupted or divided regions can reconnect scenes and give extra settling open doors. Replanting local vegetation and reestablishing normal elements assist with establishing a more neighborly climate for birds, supporting their reproducing and settling prerequisites.

5. **Contextual investigations and Examples of overcoming adversity:**

Singapore's Biodiversity Drives:

Singapore, a thickly populated city-state, has carried out different drives to upgrade metropolitan biodiversity. The incorporation of green spaces, production of bird-accommodating natural surroundings, and commitment with people in general have added to the safeguarding of settling locales for assorted bird species.

New York City's High Line:

The High Line, a changed over raised rail route in New York City, has turned into a model for metropolitan preservation. This straight park highlights assorted plantings, giving natural surroundings to birds and bugs. Such metropolitan green spaces can act as imperative passages for untamed life amidst metropolitan turn of events.

2.2 Pesticide use and its impact on swallow food sources

Swallows, famous for their elegant flight and elevated tumbling, are a gathering of birds that basically depend on bugs as their primary wellspring of food. The utilization of pesticides in farming and other human exercises has arisen as a critical danger to swallow populaces by straightforwardly affecting their vital food sources. This article investigates the complex connection between pesticide use and the downfall of swallow food sources, stressing the biological repercussions and pushing for economical practices to guarantee the prosperity of these avian species.

1. **Reliance on Bugs:**

Swallows as Ethereal Insectivores:

Swallows are named elevated insectivores, showing their specialization in catching and consuming bugs mid-flight. Their great dexterity permits them to explore through the air with striking accuracy, getting a wide assortment of flying bugs. This dietary inclination positions them as important supporters of irritation control in environments.

Effect of Bugs on Swallow Diets:

Bugs furnish swallows with fundamental supplements, including proteins and fats, significant for their endurance and conceptive achievement. The overflow and variety of flying bugs straightforwardly impact swallow populaces, influencing their wellbeing, reproducing achievement, and by and large natural job as bug regulators.

2. **Pesticides in Farming:**

Far reaching Utilization of Bug sprays:

In current agribusiness, the utilization of insect poisons has become far reaching to safeguard crops from bother pervasions. While these synthetics mean to improve crop yields, they incidentally influence non-target creatures, including helpful bugs that swallows depend on for food.

Influence on Bug Populaces:

The use of insect sprays prompts the immediate mortality of designated bothers, however it likewise has potentially negative results for non-target bugs. Advantageous bugs, like honey bees, butterflies, and different types of flying bugs, face decreases in populace because of pesticide openness. This decrease in bug overflow straightforwardly influences the accessibility of nourishment for swallows.

3. **Explicit Pesticides and their Belongings:**

Neonicotinoids:

Neonicotinoids, a class of foundational bug sprays, are generally utilized in farming. These synthetics can endure in the climate, amassing in plants and soil. Studies recommend that neonicotinoids straightforwardly hurt bugs as well as in a roundabout way influence bird populaces by lessening their prey accessibility.

Organophosphates and Carbamates:

Organophosphates and carbamates, ordinarily utilized bug sprays, can significantly affect bugs. Birds, including swallows, consuming debased prey might encounter direct damage, including neurotoxic impacts. Also, these synthetic compounds can disturb the equilibrium of bug populaces, further affecting swallow food sources.

4. **Bioaccumulation and Biomagnification:**

Gathering in Prey Species

Pesticides, once brought into the climate, can gather in the collections of bugs that swallows consume. The course of bioaccumulation brings about the grouping of these synthetic substances in the tissues of prey species, possibly arriving at levels that are unsafe to swallows over the long run.

Biomagnification through the Well established pecking order:

Biomagnification happens as pesticides climb the well established pecking order. Bugs ingest pesticides, and when swallows consume sullied bugs, the centralization of these synthetic compounds expansions in the birds. This peculiarity represents an uplifted gamble to swallows, as they might encounter more prominent openness than the bugs they go after.

5. **Influence on Conceptive Achievement:**

Eggshell Diminishing and Nestling Mortality:

Pesticide openness has been connected to conceptive difficulties in swallows. Certain pesticides, for example, organochlorines, can prompt eggshell diminishing, making eggs more vulnerable to breakage during brooding. This can bring about diminished incubating achievement and expanded nestling mortality, influencing the general efficiency of swallow populaces.

Adjusted Taking care of Conduct:

Pesticide openness might change the taking care of conduct of swallows. Birds impacted by pesticides might encounter diminished rummaging productivity, influencing their capacity to catch a sufficient amount of bugs. This compromised taking care of conduct can prompt ailing health, debilitated safe frameworks, and decreased wellness in swallow populaces.

6. **Preservation Procedures:**

Incorporated Vermin The executives (IPM):

Incorporated Bug The board (IPM) addresses a practical way to deal with bug control that limits the utilization of substance pesticides. IPM integrates a scope of methods, including organic control, crop turn, and the utilization of safe harvest assortments. By embracing IPM rehearses, ranchers can decrease the dependence on hurtful pesticides, helping the two harvests and natural life.

Cradle Zones and Natural life Cordial Cultivating:

Making support zones around agrarian fields and consolidating untamed life well disposed cultivating practices can assist with relieving the effect of pesticides on swallow food sources. These actions give shelter regions to gainful bugs, permitting them to flourish and act as an imperative food hotspot for swallows.

Without pesticide Zones:

Laying out sans pesticide zones in and around regions with high swallow action can safeguard urgent searching regions. These zones can be assigned in metropolitan, rural, and farming scenes, permitting swallows to take care of without openness to destructive synthetics.

Public Mindfulness and Promotion:

Raising public mindfulness about the effect of pesticides on swallow populaces is fundamental. Promotion endeavors can energize the reception of feasible horticultural practices, the decrease of pesticide use, and the execution of arrangements supporting untamed life amicable cultivating.

2.3 Climate change and its effects on swallow migration and breeding

Environmental change, powered by human exercises like deforestation and the consuming of petroleum derivatives, is adjusting the planet's environment at a phenomenal rate. This worldwide peculiarity significantly affects different biological systems, influencing both plant and creature species. Swallows, as transitory birds, are especially delicate to changes in environment, given their reliance on occasional examples for rearing and movement. This article digs into the complicated connection between environmental change and its impacts on swallow movement and reproducing, investigating the difficulties these avian species face and the expected ramifications for their populaces.

1. **The Meaning of Swallow Relocation and Reproducing:**

   Transient Way of behaving of Swallows:

   Swallows are known for their astounding transitory excursions, covering great many miles among reproducing and wintering grounds. Movement is a basic part of their life cycle, guaranteeing admittance to plentiful food assets and ideal rearing circumstances in various districts.

   Occasional Rearing Cycles:

   Swallows show a distinct rearing season, normally connected to the accessibility of bugs for food. Timing is urgent; a defer in relocation or reproducing can disturb the synchronization between the appearance of birds and the pinnacle accessibility of bugs, influencing the endurance of little birds.

2. **Environmental Change and its Effect on Swallow Movement:**

   Adjusted Timing of Seasons:

   Environmental change is causing shifts in the planning of seasons, with prior springs and later harvest times turning out to be more normal. These progressions can disturb the fragile harmony between the planning of swallow movements and the accessibility of food assets, possibly prompting confounds and decreased conceptive achievement.

   Temperature Changes:

   Increasing worldwide temperatures impact the way of behaving of bugs, an essential food hotspot for swallows. Hotter temperatures can speed up the development of bugs, adjusting their conveyance and overflow. Swallows, accordingly, may have to change their relocation timing to line up with these changes.

   Wind Examples and Route:

   Swallows depend on wind designs for effective significant distance trips during movement. Environmental change-actuated modifications in wind examples can affect the navigational capacities of swallows, possibly prompting longer and all the more enthusiastically exorbitant relocation courses.

3. **Rearing Difficulties in an Evolving Environment:**

   Temperature-Subordinate Nestling Development:

   The development and advancement of swallow little birds are profoundly affected by temperature and the accessibility of bug prey. Hotter temperatures might speed up the digestion of little birds, requesting expanded food consumption for ideal development. In the event that the accessibility of bugs doesn't line up with these temperature transforms, it could affect nestling endurance rates.

Outrageous Climate Occasions:

Environmental change is related with an expansion in the recurrence and force of outrageous climate occasions, including storms and heatwaves. Such occasions can negatively affect swallow homes, prompting home disappointments, primary harm, or expanded weakness of little birds to unfavorable weather patterns.

Changes in Reproducing Reaches:

Environmental change can bring about shifts in the circulation of plants and bugs, hence influencing the living spaces appropriate for swallow reproducing. Swallows might have to adjust by modifying their rearing reaches, which could prompt expanded contest for settling destinations and assets.

4. **Contextual analyses and Observational Proof:**

European Swallow (Hirundo rustica):

Concentrates on the European Swallow, a broadly concentrated on transitory species, have shown changes in appearance and takeoff dates related with environmental change. Hotter springs have prompted before appearances, affecting the planning of rearing and possibly impacting the outcome of ensuing ages.

Tree Swallow (Tachycineta bicolor):

North American Tree Swallows, known for settling in tree cavities, face difficulties as environmental change adjusts the planning of bug hatches. A confound between the pinnacle wealth of bugs and the nestling time frame can bring about decreased food accessibility for chicks, influencing their development and endurance.

5. **Transformation Systems of Swallows:**

Changes in Relocation Timing:

Swallows might show versatility in their movement timing to adjust to evolving conditions. This can include prior takeoffs from wintering grounds or postponed landings in rearing locales to more readily line up with the accessibility of food assets.

Changes in Settling Conduct:

Swallows could modify their settling conduct in light of environmental change. This could include changes in the planning of home structure, egg-laying, and nestling taking care of to upgrade conceptive progress in an evolving climate.

Changes in Rearing Reaches:

Some swallow species might answer environmental change by moving their rearing reaches to regions with additional great circumstances. This variation system, be that as it may, can prompt expanded contest for settling destinations and assets with other bird species.

6. **Preservation Suggestions:**

Safeguarding and Reestablishing Environment:

Safeguarding and reestablishing regular natural surroundings is essential for swallows confronting the difficulties of environmental change. Preservation endeavors ought to zero in on keeping up with different environments that give appropriate settling locales, plentiful bug prey, and sufficient assets for the endurance of swallow populaces.

Establishing Environment Tough Scenes:

Metropolitan and provincial scenes can be intended to be more environment strong, furnishing swallows with appropriate living spaces and limiting the effect of outrageous climate occasions. This incorporates protecting green spaces, carrying out feasible metropolitan preparation, and decreasing environment discontinuity.

Observing and Exploration:

Persistent checking and research are fundamental to comprehend the continuous effects of environmental change on swallow movement and reproducing. Long haul studies can give experiences into how various species are answering evolving conditions, directing preservation procedures and versatile administration.

7. **Worldwide Coordinated effort for Environment Activity:**

Global Preservation Arrangements:

Given the transient idea of swallows, worldwide cooperation is critical for their protection. Reinforcing and implementing peaceful accords zeroed in on environment activity and natural surroundings conservation are fundamental parts of worldwide endeavors to safeguard transient bird species.

Public Mindfulness and Backing:

Raising public mindfulness about the effect of environmental change on swallow relocation and reproducing is imperative. Public help for strategies tending to environmental change, maintainable practices, and protection endeavors can add to establishing a stronger and versatile climate for swallows.

2.4Introduction of invasive species and competition for resources

The presentation of obtrusive species has arisen as a huge driver of biological change, disturbing normal environments and setting off serious contest for assets. Obtrusive species, frequently presented deliberately or coincidentally by human exercises, can outcompete local verdure, prompting uneven characters with broad results. This article investigates the perplexing elements of intrusive species presentation, the natural effects of asset contest, and the difficulties related with overseeing and moderating these results.

1. **Figuring out Obtrusive Species:**
   Definition and Qualities:
   Obtrusive species are non-local organic entities that, when acquainted with another climate, secure themselves and multiply quickly, frequently hurting the environment. These species show attributes like high conceptive rates, versatility, and productive asset use, permitting them to outcompete local species.
   Pathways of Presentation:
   Obtrusive species can be presented through different pathways, including deliberate presentations for agrarian or elaborate purposes, unplanned presentations through exchange and transport, and regular reach extensions because of environmental change. Human exercises, especially globalization, assume a huge part in working with the spread of obtrusive species.

2. **Rivalry for Assets:**
   Asset Specialties and Use:
   Obtrusive species frequently exploit vacant or underutilized asset specialties in the new climate. This incorporates admittance to daylight, water, supplements, and other basic assets that local species rely upon. The productive use of these assets by intrusive species can prompt extreme contest with local partners.
   Influence on Local Biodiversity:
   The opposition for assets among intrusive and local species can significantly affect biodiversity. Obtrusive species may outcompete local vegetation, prompting declines or eliminations of weak species. This disturbance in biodiversity can have flowing consequences for environment construction and capability.

3. **Biological Effects of Obtrusive Species:**
   Adjusted Environment Elements:
   The presentation of obtrusive species can disturb regular environment elements. Obtrusive plants, for instance, may modify fire systems, supplement cycling, and water accessibility, prompting changes in the piece and design of local plant networks.
   Predation and Rivalry:
   Intrusive creatures frequently apply predation strain on local species or straightforwardly seek food assets. This can bring about populace declines or social changes in local species, influencing the equilibrium of hunter prey connections and local area cooperations.
   Living space Debasement:
   Intrusive species can add to living space corruption by changing soil structure, supplement levels, and vegetation piece. This corruption, thusly, influences

the appropriateness of the climate for local species, prompting decreases in their overflow and circulation.

4. **Instances of Obtrusive Species and Asset Contest:**

Zebra Mussels (Dreissena polymorpha):

Zebra mussels, local to Eastern Europe, were unexpectedly acquainted with North America in balance water from ships. Their fast multiplication in freshwater biological systems has prompted rivalry with local mussels for food assets and connection destinations. Zebra mussels channel a lot of water, influencing local microscopic fish populaces and modifying supplement cycling.

Stick Frogs (Rhinella marina):

Initially acquainted with control bothers in sugarcane ranches in Australia, stick frogs have turned into an exceptionally obtrusive animal groups. Their poisonous skin discharges safeguard them from predation, permitting them to outcompete local creatures of land and water for assets. This has prompted decreases in local frog populaces and disturbances in nearby environments.

5. **The board Difficulties and Systems:**

Early Location and Quick Reaction:

Identifying and answering obtrusive species right off the bat in their foundation is critical for successful administration. Quick reaction systems, including quarantine measures, destruction endeavors, and public mindfulness crusades, can forestall additionally spread and moderate the effects of obtrusive species.

Organic Control:

Organic control includes the presentation of regular hunters, parasites, or microorganisms to control intrusive species. Cautious thought and chance appraisal are fundamental to keep away from potentially negative results and guarantee the progress of organic control measures.

Substance Control:

The utilization of substance control, like herbicides and pesticides, can be utilized to oversee intrusive species. Notwithstanding, this approach requires cautious thought to limit damage to non-target species and environments. Coordinated bother the board systems that join compound control with different techniques are in many cases more viable.

Reclamation and Restoration:

Reestablishing and restoring environments impacted by obtrusive species is a long haul and complex interaction. This might include the expulsion of intrusive species, natural surroundings rebuilding, and renewed introduction of local species. Achievement frequently relies upon a mix of natural information, local area commitment, and supported endeavors.

6. **Worldwide Points of view on Intrusive Species The executives:**

Global Joint effort:

Obtrusive species know no international limits, and powerful administration frequently requires global cooperation. Associations like the Show on Natural Variety (CBD) and territorial drives work with the trading of data, assets, and best practices for intrusive species the executives.

Island Biological systems and Biosecurity:

Island biological systems are especially powerless against obtrusive species, as numerous island species advanced in detachment and need normal safeguards against presented dangers. Executing severe biosecurity measures, including quarantine conventions and assessment of approaching merchandise, is fundamental for safeguarding island biodiversity.

7. **Environmental Change and Obtrusive Species Elements:**

Changed Territory Reasonableness:

Environmental change can impact the circulation and overflow of obtrusive species by adjusting territory appropriateness. As temperature and precipitation designs shift, already ungracious regions might become helpful for the foundation and spread of obtrusive species.

Expanded Recurrence of Intrusions:

Environmental change might build the recurrence of obtrusive species presentations and foundation. Hotter temperatures and changes in precipitation can make better circumstances for the endurance and expansion of obtrusive species in new conditions.

Synergistic Consequences for Biological systems:

The consolidated effects of environmental change and obtrusive species can synergistically affect biological systems. For instance, obtrusive plant species might flourish in changed climatic circumstances, fueling living space corruption and rivalry with local species.

8. **Public Mindfulness and Schooling:**

Forestalling Further Presentations:

Public mindfulness and schooling assume a urgent part in forestalling further presentations of obtrusive species. Figuring out the results of delivering non-local species into the wild and taking on capable pet possession rehearses are key parts of forestalling accidental presentations.

Resident Science and Observing:

Connecting with people in general in resident science drives and checking projects can contribute significant information on the spread and effect of obtrusive species. Enabling people group to effectively partake in obtrusive species the executives cultivates a feeling of stewardship and aggregate liability.

Chapter 3

Conservation Strategies

Notwithstanding mounting natural difficulties, preservation procedures assume a crucial part in defending the rich embroidery of life on The planet. Biodiversity, the assortment of life in the entirety of its structures, is under danger from environment misfortune, environmental change, contamination, and the presentation of obtrusive species. This article investigates a thorough scope of protection procedures, from living space safeguarding and reclamation to local area commitment and global cooperation. By tending to the underlying drivers of biodiversity decline and advancing economical practices, these techniques intend to make an agreeable harmony between human exercises and the normal world.

1. **Territory Protection and Reclamation:**

   Safeguarded Regions and Stores:

   Laying out and keeping up with safeguarded regions and stores is a principal protection procedure. These assigned spaces go about as safe-havens for a different cluster of animal groups, giving undisturbed territories where widely varied vegetation can flourish. Legitimate administration, requirement of guidelines, and continuous observing are urgent parts of this procedure.

   Territory Availability:

   Guaranteeing availability between natural surroundings is fundamental for permitting the development of species, keeping up with hereditary variety, and supporting environmental cycles. Passage creation, untamed life extensions, and environment rebuilding projects add to laying out and improving network, alleviating the effect of territory discontinuity.

   Reforestation and Afforestation:

   Reforestation and afforestation drives center around establishing trees and reestablishing forested regions that have been debased or lost. These activities add to carbon sequestration, support biodiversity, and improve biological system administrations. Local area contribution in tree establishing programs advances a feeling of responsibility and stewardship.

2. **Feasible Asset The board:**

Supportable Fishing Practices:

Overfishing is a critical danger to marine biodiversity. Executing manageable fishing rehearses, for example, share frameworks, size restricts, and safeguarded marine regions, keeps up with fish populaces at levels that help environment wellbeing and forestall the breakdown of fisheries.

Regenerative Farming:

Farming is a significant driver of natural surroundings misfortune and corruption. Changing to regenerative horticultural practices, for example, agroforestry and cover editing, advances soil wellbeing, diminishes the requirement for compound sources of info, and jelly biodiversity inside and around farmlands.

Certificate Projects:

Accreditations like Rainforest Union and Backwoods Stewardship Gathering (FSC) guarantee that items meet specific natural and social supportability guidelines. Supporting and advancing these affirmations empowers capable asset the board and assists shoppers with settling on ecologically cognizant decisions.

3. **Obtrusive Species The board:**

Early Location and Quick Reaction:

Early location of intrusive species is basic for forestalling their foundation and spread. Quick reaction measures, including quarantine, destruction, and public mindfulness crusades, can really contain intrusive species before they actually hurt.

Organic Control:

Presenting normal hunters, parasites, or microbes to control obtrusive species is a natural control procedure. Nonetheless, cautious gamble appraisal is urgent to stay away from potentially negative side-effects, and nonstop checking is important to guarantee the progress of these control measures.

Mechanical and Compound Control:

Mechanical strategies, like manual expulsion or the utilization of apparatus, and substance control, including the designated use of herbicides or pesticides, can be utilized to oversee intrusive species. These techniques ought to be specific, limiting mischief to non-target species and biological systems.

4. **Environmental Change Moderation and Transformation:**

Environmentally friendly power Change:

Progressing from petroleum derivatives to sustainable power sources, for example, sun oriented and wind power, is a vital stage in relieving environmental change. Lessening ozone depleting substance discharges eases back the speed of a worldwide temperature alteration, giving biological systems and species additional opportunity to adjust.

Environment Versatile Foundation:

Planning and carrying out environment strong foundation limits the effect of outrageous climate occasions on biological systems. This incorporates methodologies like green framework, which utilizes regular cycles to oversee water and decrease the gamble of flooding, helping both human networks and biodiversity.

Helped Relocation:

Helped relocation includes effectively moving species to additional appropriate living spaces because of environmental change. While a questionable system, it very well might be important to assist species with adjusting to quickly evolving conditions, especially when normal movement is upset by human turn of events.

5. **Local area Commitment and Schooling:**

Ecological Instruction Projects:

Instructing people group about the significance of biodiversity, biological systems, and maintainable practices encourages a feeling of natural stewardship. Ecological training programs in schools, public venues, and online stages engage people to put forth informed decisions that add to preservation attempts.

Neighborhood Strengthening and Possession:

Including neighborhood networks in protection drives upgrades the achievement and manageability of undertakings. Enabling people group to effectively partake in navigation, supportable asset the board, and eco-the travel industry drives makes a common obligation regarding protecting biodiversity.

Native Information and Practices:

Perceiving and regarding native information and practices is fundamental for powerful protection. Native people group frequently have important experiences into feasible asset the board and biodiversity preservation, and cooperative organizations can incorporate customary thinking with present day protection systems.

6. **Innovation and Advancement:**

Observing and Observation:

Innovation, like satellite symbolism, robots, and camera traps, helps with checking biodiversity, identifying changes in environments, and following the developments of natural life. These devices give significant information to preservation arranging and navigation.

Hereditary Protection and Cryopreservation:

Hereditary protection techniques, including seed banks, cryopreservation, and tissue culture, assist with safeguarding the hereditary variety of plant species.

These actions go about as protection against termination and backing future rebuilding endeavors.

Resident Science and Publicly supporting:

Connecting with residents in logical exploration through resident science drives and publicly supporting activities grows information assortment abilities. Volunteers can add to biodiversity observing, obtrusive species announcing, and other examination endeavors, upgrading the extension and adequacy of preservation programs.

7. **Worldwide Coordinated effort:**

Worldwide Preservation Arrangements:

Worldwide joint effort is indispensable for tending to worldwide preservation challenges. Arrangements like the Show on Natural Variety (CBD) and the Paris Settlement on environmental change give structures to composed activity and asset dividing between countries.

Transboundary Protection Drives:

Numerous species have ranges that length different nations. Transboundary preservation drives include cooperation between adjoining countries to oversee shared biological systems, safeguard transient species, and address normal protection challenges.

Worldwide Exploration Organizations:

Building worldwide examination networks works with the trading of information and mastery. Cooperative endeavors among researchers, specialists, and protection experts improve how we might interpret biodiversity, environment elements, and the adequacy of preservation procedures.

8. **Monetary Motivations and Financial Apparatuses:**

Installments for Environment Administrations (PES):

Installments for Environment Administrations programs give monetary impetuses to landowners or networks for keeping up with or reestablishing biological systems that offer important types of assistance, like carbon sequestration, water decontamination, or natural surroundings conservation.

Eco-Accreditations and Feasible Exchange:

Eco-affirmations, similar to the Woods Stewardship Gathering (FSC) certificate for reasonably oversaw woodlands, make monetary motivations for organizations to take on earth mindful practices. Supporting reasonably created merchandise empowers a market shift towards more mindful and preservation well disposed items.

Monetary Valuation of Environment Administrations:

Appointing financial worth to biological system administrations, like fertilization, water filtration, and environment guideline, assists policymakers and organizations with perceiving the substantial advantages of biodiversity preservation. This approach coordinates natural contemplations into monetary direction.

9. **Difficulties and Future Standpoint:**

Fracture and Environment Misfortune:

Progressing environment fracture and misfortune keep on presenting huge difficulties to protection endeavors. Urbanization, horticulture extension, and foundation advancement add to the corruption and confinement of biological systems.

Environmental Change Vulnerabilities:

The vulnerabilities related with environmental change, including the rate and size of temperature increments, ocean level ascent, and outrageous climate occasions, present difficulties for preservation arranging. Transformation systems should stay adaptable to oblige changing environment situations.

Political Will and Strategy Execution:

Accomplishing fruitful protection results requires political will and the powerful execution of arrangements. Fortifying natural guidelines, upholding safeguarded region the executives, and tending to underlying drivers of biodiversity misfortune are fundamental parts of compelling preservation strategy.

Obtrusive Species and Arising Dangers:

The proceeded with spread of obtrusive species and the development of new dangers, like sicknesses and novel poisons, request versatile and inventive protection procedures. Proactive measures, quick reaction plans, and examination into arising dangers are basic for future biodiversity protection.

3.1Habitat preservation and restoration

Natural surroundings protection and rebuilding are urgent procedures in the preservation tool compartment, pointed toward shielding biodiversity and advancing environmental versatility. These methodologies address the steadily developing dangers presented by human exercises, like urbanization, deforestation, and contamination, which add to the misfortune and corruption of normal environments around the world.

Environment Safeguarding:

Protecting flawless territories is a foundation of preservation endeavors. Laying out safeguarded regions and natural life saves keeps up with the environmental equilibrium and gives places of refuge to assorted plant and creature species. These regions go about as shelters where untamed life can raise, feed, and complete normal ways of behaving without the prompt dangers presented by human infringement or asset extraction.

Key preservation arranging includes recognizing and assigning areas of high biodiversity importance as safeguarded zones. These regions might incorporate tropical rainforests, wetlands, coral reefs, and other basic environments. Severe guidelines and the executives plans administer these zones, guaranteeing that human exercises inside them are supportable and viable with the drawn out soundness of the natural surroundings.

Natural surroundings Rebuilding:

Territory rebuilding endeavors become possibly the most important factor when environments have been debased or changed because of human exercises or normal occasions. Reclamation expects to renew biological systems, once again introduce local species, and reproduce practical territories that help biodiversity.

Reforestation and afforestation projects center around recharging tree cover in regions where deforestation has happened. This sequesters carbon as well as gives living spaces to a bunch of animal varieties. Wetland reclamation includes reproducing or restoring wetland environments, which are basic for water filtration, flood control, and filling in as nurseries for the overwhelming majority amphibian species.

Effective living space rebuilding requires a profound comprehension of the biological system's normal cycles, the recognizable proof of key species, and cautious intending to impersonate the circumstances fundamental for the arrival of local verdure. Moreover, people group inclusion is many times indispensable to rebuilding projects, encouraging a feeling of responsibility and responsibility among neighborhood inhabitants.

The Cooperative energy among Safeguarding and Rebuilding:

While environment safeguarding and rebuilding are unmistakable techniques, they frequently work pair. Safeguarded territories act as reference focuses for figuring out the normal condition of environments, directing rebuilding endeavors. Besides, reestablished natural surroundings add to the availability of scenes, guaranteeing that species can move uninhibitedly between safeguarded regions, advancing hereditary variety and variation.

1. **Creating artificial nesting sites**

   Making fake settling locales is a proactive preservation measure intended to address territory misfortune and backing declining untamed life populaces. Frequently executed for species like birds, bats, and turtles, these designs emulate normal natural surroundings to give places of refuge to reproducing and cover. Bird enclosures, bat boxes, and fake reefs are instances of such drives. These endeavors not just assistance make up for the deficiency of normal settling destinations because of urbanization or living space annihilation yet additionally add to the general protection of biodiversity by cultivating the conceptive achievement and endurance of weak species in human-modified scenes.

2. **Establishing protected areas for breeding and feeding**

Laying out safeguarded regions for rearing and taking care of is a fundamental protection technique. These assigned zones, enveloping different environments like wetlands, woodlands, and marine natural surroundings, give a safe-haven to untamed life during basic life stages. Severe guidelines oversee human exercises inside these areas, guaranteeing insignificant unsettling influence to rearing and taking care of ways of behaving. Such safeguarded spaces go about as fundamental shelters, supporting the endurance of various species by shielding their regenerative cycles and guaranteeing a bountiful and undisturbed stockpile of food assets. This system advances biodiversity protection, offering an outline for orchestrating human exercises with the necessities of the regular world.

3.2 Reducing pesticide use and promoting alternative farming practices

Current horticulture, while fundamental for taking care of a developing worldwide populace, frequently depends vigorously on pesticides to control bothers and boost yields. In any case, the exorbitant utilization of these synthetic specialists has raised critical ecological and wellbeing concerns. Accordingly, a shift towards diminishing pesticide reliance and embracing elective cultivating rehearses has turned into a basic component chasing maintainable farming.

Difficulties of Pesticide Reliance:

Natural Effect:

Pesticides, intended to kill or control bothers, can have unseen side-effects on non-target creatures and biological systems. Spillover from fields can pollute water sources, hurting amphibian life, and adding to the improvement of pesticide-safe species.

Human Wellbeing Concerns:

Drawn out openness to pesticides presents wellbeing dangers to horticultural laborers and close by networks. Respiratory issues, skin problems, and long haul wellbeing suggestions have been connected to the utilization of specific pesticides. Limiting openness and advancing more secure choices are central for human prosperity.

Loss of Biodiversity:

Pesticides, while focusing on unambiguous bugs, may coincidentally hurt valuable bugs, birds, and other untamed life. This disturbance yet to be determined of biological systems can prompt decreases in pollinator populaces, soil wellbeing corruption, and generally loss of biodiversity.

Advancing Decreased Pesticide Use:

Incorporated Bug The executives (IPM):

Incorporated Bug The executives is an all encompassing methodology that consolidates different procedures to oversee bothers productively while limiting the utilization of synthetic pesticides. Strategies incorporate organic control (presenting regular hunters), crop revolution, and the utilization of safe yield assortments.

IPM means to keep up with bother populaces at levels that don't cause monetary harm, lessening the dependence on compound intercessions.

Crop Turn and Expansion:

Crop turn upsets the existence patterns of bugs and sicknesses, decreasing the requirement for substance controls. Differentiating crops inside a locale likewise adds to bother the executives, as specific nuisances are intended for specific harvests. This approach cultivates a stronger and adjusted agroecosystem.

Cover Yields and Green Compost:

Cover yields and green compost improve soil ripeness as well as go about as regular vermin suppressants. They give territory to valuable bugs, further develop soil structure, and diminish the requirement for engineered manures and pesticides. This regenerative methodology advances a better and more manageable rural framework.

Elective Cultivating Practices:

Natural Cultivating:

Natural cultivating underlines the utilization of normal data sources and strategies to develop crops. Staying away from engineered pesticides, herbicides, and hereditarily changed creatures, natural cultivating depends on practices like harvest pivot, fertilizing the soil, and organic vermin control. This strategy means to deliver nutritious, synthetic free food while focusing on soil wellbeing and biodiversity.

Agroecology:

Agroecology incorporates environmental standards into agrarian frameworks, underlining biodiversity, supplement cycling, and normal bug control. By imitating regular biological systems, agroecological approaches improve flexibility to vermin and sicknesses, lessen the requirement for outside inputs, and advance manageable cultivating rehearses.

Accuracy Farming:

Accuracy farming use innovation, including sensors, robots, and GPS, to enhance asset use and limit natural effect. By exactly focusing on inputs like water, composts, and pesticides, ranchers can increment productivity, diminish squander, and relieve the natural impression of agribusiness.

Difficulties and Boundaries:

Information and Schooling:

Ranchers might confront boundaries in taking on elective practices because of an absence of information, mindfulness, or admittance to data. Instructive projects and expansion administrations are urgent for spreading data about feasible cultivating procedures and their advantages.

Introductory Expenses and Change Period:

Changing from regular to elective cultivating practices might include introductory expenses and changes. Ranchers might require support during this progress period, including monetary motivations, specialized help, and admittance to business sectors for reasonably created products.

Market Interest and Accreditation:

Empowering market interest for reasonably delivered rural items is fundamental. Accreditation programs that check adherence to economical practices can give motivators to ranchers and fabricate customer trust in the biological uprightness of the food they buy.

Government Arrangements and Backing:

Endowment Change:

States can change agrarian appropriations to boost maintainable practices and deter inordinate pesticide use. Diverting appropriations towards agroecological approaches and offering monetary help for the progress to economical cultivating can be instrumental.

Innovative work Subsidizing:

Expanded subsidizing for innovative work in economical agribusiness can drive advancement and the reception of elective practices. Supporting examination into strong yield assortments, natural bug control techniques, and maintainable cultivating advancements adds to long haul horticultural maintainability.

Administrative Measures:

Fortifying guidelines connected with pesticide use, water quality, and soil wellbeing can advance dependable agrarian practices. Executing and implementing strategies that focus on ecological protection and human wellbeing are critical for a fruitful change to feasible horticulture.

3.3Climate change mitigation and adaptation strategies

Environmental change, energized by human exercises and the discharge of ozone depleting substances, presents phenomenal difficulties to our planet's biological systems and social orders. To address this worldwide emergency, a two dimensional methodology including both moderation and variation procedures is fundamental. These methodologies point not exclusively to check the continuous effects of environmental change yet additionally to construct flexibility even with unavoidable changes.

Environmental Change Alleviation:

Change to Environmentally friendly power:

The foundation of environmental change alleviation is the shift from petroleum derivatives to sustainable power sources. Tackling the force of sunlight based, wind, hydro, and geothermal energy diminishes reliance on carbon-concentrated energy creation, controling ozone depleting substance emanations answerable for an Earth-wide temperature boost.

Energy Effectiveness:

Further developing energy effectiveness in different areas, from transportation to assembling, diminishes generally energy utilization and mitigates emanations.

This incorporates the improvement of energy-productive advancements, maintainable metropolitan preparation, and the reception of eco-accommodating practices in ventures.

Afforestation and Reforestation:

Trees assume a pivotal part in sequestering carbon dioxide from the climate. Afforestation (establishing trees in new regions) and reforestation (replanting in deforested regions) upgrade carbon catch, add to biodiversity protection, and advance reasonable land the executives rehearses.

Carbon Catch and Capacity (CCS):

CCS advances catch carbon dioxide outflows delivered from ventures and power plants, keeping them from entering the air. Put away underground, this innovation diminishes the grouping of ozone harming substances, moderating the effect of environmental change.

Environmental Change Variation:

Versatile Framework:

Planning and carrying out versatile framework can endure the effects of environmental change, including outrageous climate occasions, rising ocean levels, and changing precipitation designs. This includes developing structures, streets, and other framework considering environment flexibility.

Water The board:

Environmental change frequently prompts modified precipitation designs, influencing water accessibility and expanding the recurrence of outrageous climate occasions. Carrying out maintainable water the executives rehearses, for example, water reaping, further developing water system productivity, and safeguarding water sources, assists networks with adjusting to evolving conditions.

Crop Enhancement and Supportable Farming:

Changing environment designs influence farming, undermining food security. Crop broadening, establishing tough assortments, and taking on manageable rural practices upgrade the versatility of cultivating frameworks. Agroecological approaches elevate flexibility to climatic varieties while guaranteeing economical food creation.

Early Admonition Frameworks:

Creating and executing successful early admonition frameworks is critical for limiting the effect of environment related debacles. Convenient cautions empower networks to empty, plan for outrageous climate occasions, and diminish the death toll and property.

Incorporated Systems:

Environment Based Transformation:

Environment based transformation includes using regular biological systems to upgrade flexibility. This incorporates the reclamation and preservation of wetlands, mangroves, and timberlands, which offer fundamental types of assistance, for example, flood control, water sanitization, and environment insurance.

Local area Commitment and Schooling:

Engaging people group with information about environmental change, its effects, and versatile techniques cultivates strength at the neighborhood level. Local area drove drives, participatory preparation, and the reconciliation of conventional information add to compelling variation.

Worldwide Coordinated effort:

Environmental change knows no boundaries, requiring worldwide coordinated effort. Peaceful accords, like the Paris Understanding, give a system to nations to cooperate, share information, and dispense assets for both relief and variation endeavors.

Challenges and the Way Forward:

Asset Designation:

The designation of monetary assets for both moderation and transformation procedures stays a test. Adjusting ventures between discharge decrease innovations and building environment versatile foundation is pivotal for a far reaching environment procedure.

Value and Equity:

Weak people group frequently endure the worst part of environmental change influences notwithstanding contributing the least to worldwide emanations. Resolving issues of value and equity is fundamental in environment transformation and alleviation endeavors, guaranteeing that the most impacted networks get satisfactory help.

Advancement and Exploration:

Continuous advancement and examination are basic for growing new innovations, refining existing techniques, and adjusting to arising environment challenges. Interests in environment science and innovation can prepare for more compelling and proficient alleviation and variation arrangements.

3.4 Invasive species management and control measures

Obtrusive species, frequently presented by human exercises, represent a huge danger to biodiversity and biological system security. These non-local creatures can outcompete and uproot local species, prompting environmental lopsided characteristics and territory debasement. Intrusive species the board includes a scope of techniques pointed toward forestalling, controlling, and relieving the effects of these natural trespassers. This extensive investigation digs into the different control measures, challenges, and imaginative methodologies utilized in obtrusive species the executives.

1. **Grasping Obtrusive Species:**

Definition and Qualities:

Obtrusive species are non-local creatures that lay out and multiply in new conditions, frequently hurting local environments. Their prosperity is credited to attributes like quick multiplication, versatility, and productive asset usage, permitting them to outcompete local verdure.

Pathways of Presentation:

Intrusive species can enter new conditions through assorted pathways, including deliberate presentations for agribusiness or fancy purposes, unintentional presentations through exchange and transport, and normal reach extensions because of environmental change. Human exercises assume a significant part in working with the spread of obtrusive species worldwide.

2. **Effects of Obtrusive Species:**

Biodiversity Misfortune:

Obtrusive species can outcompete local species for assets, prompting declines or eradications of weak vegetation. This disturbance in biodiversity can have flowing consequences for environment construction and capability.

Territory Debasement:

Obtrusive species frequently adjust environment construction and organization, prompting corruption. This can remember changes for soil piece, supplement cycling, and vegetation cover, adversely influencing the appropriateness of the climate for local species.

Monetary Results:

Obtrusive species can have huge financial effects by influencing agribusiness, fisheries, and ranger service. Crop misfortune, diminished yields, and harm to foundation are among the financial results related with specific intrusive species.

3. **Intrusive Species The executives Approaches:**

Avoidance:

Avoidance is the principal line of guard against obtrusive species. This includes measures like severe biosecurity conventions, quarantine guidelines, and public mindfulness missions to limit the unexpected presentation and spread of obtrusive species.

Early Location and Fast Reaction:

Identifying and answering obtrusive species right off the bat in their foundation is urgent for compelling administration. Quick reaction systems incorporate annihilation endeavors, quarantine measures, and public commitment to forestall additionally spread.

Natural Control:

Natural control includes presenting regular hunters, parasites, or microorganisms to control intrusive species. Cautious thought and hazard appraisal are fundamental to stay away from potentially negative side-effects and guarantee the progress of organic control measures.

Mechanical and Compound Control:

Mechanical techniques, like manual evacuation or the utilization of hardware, and substance control, including the designated use of herbicides or pesticides, can be utilized to oversee obtrusive species. These techniques ought to be particular to limit damage to non-target species and biological systems.

4. **Avoidance Systems:**

Severe Biosecurity Measures:

Forestalling the presentation of intrusive species starts with severe biosecurity measures. This includes observing and directing the development of products, vehicles, and freight to limit the accidental vehicle of obtrusive species across borders.

Quarantine Conventions:

Carrying out viable quarantine conventions is pivotal for forestalling the spread of intrusive species. Quarantine measures are applied to imported products, plants, and creatures to guarantee that potential trespassers are identified and tended to before they lay out in another climate.

Public Mindfulness and Schooling:

Public mindfulness and schooling efforts assume a key part in forestalling the unexpected presentation of obtrusive species. Illuminating general society about the dangers related with specific ways of behaving, for example, delivering fascinating pets into the wild, forestalls the spread of obtrusive species.

5. **Early Location and Fast Reaction:**

Reconnaissance and Observing Projects:

Early location depends on complete reconnaissance and observing projects. These projects include ordinary assessments, reviews, and information assortment to distinguish the presence of obtrusive species in their beginning phases of foundation.

Resident Science Drives:

Drawing in people in general in resident science drives upgrades the extent of early discovery endeavors. Resident researchers can contribute important information through perceptions and announcing, helping with the distinguishing proof and following of obtrusive species.

Quick Reaction Groups:

Laying out quick reaction groups furnished with the instruments and skill to address obtrusive species is basic. These groups can rapidly activate to contain and destroy recently recognized intrusive species, forestalling additionally spread and limiting natural harm.

6. **Organic Control:**

Regular Hunters and Parasitoids:

Presenting regular hunters or parasitoids well defined for the obtrusive species can assist with controlling their populaces. This approach depends on the guideline of outfitting normal environmental connections to accomplish a harmony between the trespasser and its regular foes.

Microorganisms and Sicknesses:

Presenting microorganisms or sicknesses that explicitly target intrusive species can be a viable natural control methodology. This strategy is painstakingly investigated and checked to guarantee that it specifically influences the objective intruder without hurting non-target species.

Specific Herbivory:

A few intrusive plants can be constrained by presenting herbivores that specifically feed on them. This technique, known as specific herbivory, use the normal taking care of inclinations of specific creatures to oversee intrusive plant species.

7. **Mechanical and Synthetic Control:**

Manual Evacuation

Manual evacuation includes actually eliminating intrusive species from the climate. This can incorporate hand-pulling weeds, physically chopping down plants, or catching and eliminating obtrusive creatures. While work concentrated, manual expulsion is frequently successful for restricted invasions.

Mechanical Hardware:

Mechanical hardware, like trimmers, dredgers, or oceanic collectors, can be utilized to control obtrusive vegetation. This strategy is appropriate for huge scope pervasions and is many times utilized in regions where manual evacuation is unreasonable.

Herbicides and Pesticides:

The utilization of herbicides and pesticides is a typical synthetic control strategy for overseeing intrusive species. Cautious thought is given to choosing synthetics that explicitly focus on the intrusive species while limiting damage to non-target living beings and the climate.

Coordinated Vermin The executives (IPM):

Incorporated Irritation The executives (IPM) is an all encompassing methodology that consolidates different control strategies, including organic, mechanical, and synthetic measures. IPM plans to accomplish successful nuisance control while limiting ecological effect and diminishing dependence on substance intercessions.

8. **Challenges in Obtrusive Species The board:**

Absence of Financing and Assets:

Obtrusive species the executives requires huge monetary assets, and deficient subsidizing can thwart successful control endeavors. Getting supported subsidizing for examination, checking, and on-the-ground the executives is critical for progress.

Globalization and Exchange:

Globalization works with the accidental presentation of intrusive species through exchange and travel. Tending to the pathways of presentation, especially with regards to worldwide exchange, is trying because of the sheer volume of merchandise and development of individuals.

Slack Time in Recognition:

Intrusive species frequently make some slack memories among presentation and recognition, permitting them to lay out and spread before viable control measures can be carried out. Further developing early location techniques and reaction times is a persistent test.

Protection from Control Measures:

An obtrusive animal categories can foster protection from control measures, including herbicides or natural controls. This versatility highlights the requirement for progressing research and versatile administration systems.

9. **Imaginative Methodologies in Obtrusive Species The board:**

Quality Altering Advances:

Quality altering advances, like CRISPR-Cas9, offer expected roads for designated control of intrusive species. Research is progressing to investigate the plausibility of utilizing quality altering to present attributes that limit the obtrusiveness of specific species.

Independent Innovations:

Independent innovations, including drones and mechanical frameworks, are progressively being utilized for observing and overseeing intrusive species. These advancements give proficient and practical method for looking over huge regions and carrying out control measures.

Environmental Rebuilding and Rewilding:

Underscoring natural reclamation and rewilding can assist with reestablishing local territories, making them stronger to intrusive species. By making conditions good for local greenery, reclamation endeavors add to the general wellbeing and biodiversity of environments.

Chapter 4

Citizen Science And Community Involvement

Resident science and local area contribution have arisen as useful assets in the domain of natural preservation, changing the manner in which we comprehend and address complex biological difficulties. As a comprehensive methodology, these drives influence the aggregate force of people to contribute important information, experiences, and activities that benefit logical exploration and neighborhood protection endeavors. This investigation dives into the standards, effect, difficulties, and capability of resident science and local area contribution in encouraging a feeling of ecological stewardship and driving good change.

1. **Grasping Resident Science:**

   Definition and Standards:

   Resident science includes the dynamic support of general society in logical exploration. People, frequently alluded to as resident researchers, team up with researchers and specialists to gather information, direct analyses, or add to logical ventures. This comprehensive methodology democratizes logical request, permitting non-experts to connect definitively in the logical cycle.

   Sorts of Resident Science Tasks:

   Resident science projects differ generally in extension and concentration. They can incorporate environmental checking, biodiversity studies, environment perceptions, stargazing, and, surprisingly, the examination of enormous datasets through internet based stages. The variety of undertakings mirrors the flexibility of resident science to various logical disciplines.

2. **The Job of Local area Contribution:**

   Local area Based Protection:

   Local area contribution in ecological preservation stretches out past information assortment and examination. It envelops cooperative endeavors where neighborhood networks effectively partake in the dynamic cycle, arranging, and execution of preservation drives. This comprehensive methodology perceives the interconnectedness of networks with their surroundings.

Neighborhood Information and Mastery:

Networks have important neighborhood information about biological systems, natural life conduct, and ecological changes. Coordinating this native information with logical skill improves the viability of preservation projects, encouraging a comprehensive comprehension of environments.

3. **Standards of Fruitful Resident Science and Local area Inclusion:**

Openness and Inclusivity:

Fruitful resident science projects focus on availability, guaranteeing that co-operation is available to people of assorted foundations, ages, and ability levels. This inclusivity widens the pool of patrons, enhancing the information gathered and encouraging a more different academic local area.

Clear Targets and Correspondence:

Obvious task goals and clear correspondence are fundamental for connecting with resident researchers and local area individuals. Straightforward correspondence fabricates trust and engages members by giving an unmistakable comprehension of the undertaking's objectives, strategies, and anticipated results.

Preparing and Backing:

Giving sufficient preparation and backing is vital for guaranteeing the nature of information gathered. This might include studios, online assets, or mentorship programs that engage members with the vital abilities and information to definitively contribute.

4. **Effect of Resident Science and Local area Inclusion:**

Logical Commitments:

Resident science has demonstrated to be an important resource in logical exploration, growing the scale and extent of information assortment. From observing bird movements to following changes in plant phenology, resident researchers add to an abundance of data that helps researchers in resolving squeezing natural inquiries.

Neighborhood Protection Examples of overcoming adversity:

Local area contribution in protection drives has prompted various examples of overcoming adversity around the world. From reforestation projects driven by neighborhood networks to the foundation of local area oversaw marine saves, the dynamic support of networks has exhibited the potential for reasonable and powerful preservation results.

Schooling and Mindfulness:

Resident science and local area association add to ecological training and mindfulness. Support in logical examination improves' comprehension people might interpret biological cycles, cultivates a feeling of association with nature, and urges a proactive way to deal with ecological difficulties.

5. **Instances of Resident Science Undertakings:**

eBird:

eBird is a broadly perceived resident science project that spotlights on bird-watching and bird information assortment. Givers, going from easygoing bird fans to enthusiastic ornithologists, submit bird perceptions through the eBird stage, adding to a worldwide information base utilized for avian examination and protection.

NASA Globe Eyewitness:

The NASA Globe Eyewitness project connects with resident researchers in checking Earth's environments. Members utilize their cell phones to gather information ashore cover, tree level, and mosquito natural surroundings, giving significant data to logical examination on environment, biodiversity, and general wellbeing.

Zooniverse:

Zooniverse is a stage facilitating an assortment of online resident science projects across various disciplines. From arranging universes and distinguishing creature ways of behaving in camera trap pictures to translating authentic records, Zooniverse permits members to add to assorted research attempts.

6. **Challenges in Resident Science and Local area Association:**

Information Quality and Normalization:

Keeping up with information quality and guaranteeing normalization across assorted supporters can challenge. Changeability in perception abilities and techniques might present irregularities, requiring strong approval cycles to maintain the dependability of resident science information.

Maintainability and Long haul Commitment:

Supporting interest and commitment over the drawn out represents a test for some resident science projects. Guaranteeing progressing investment requires inventive systems, persistent correspondence, and endeavors to perceive and praise the commitments of members.

Value and Inclusivity:

Accomplishing value and inclusivity in resident science can challenge, with specific socioeconomics being underrepresented. Addressing boundaries connected with access, social responsiveness, and financial elements is fundamental for cultivating a different and comprehensive resident science local area.

7. **Best Practices and Suggestions:**

Local area Driven Approach:

Embracing a local area driven approach in preservation projects includes teaming up intimately with neighborhood networks, perceiving their requirements and yearnings, and coordinating conventional information into logical practices. This approach encourages a feeling of pride and aggregate liability regarding natural stewardship.

Innovation and Availability:

Utilizing innovation upgrades the openness and reach of resident science projects. Versatile applications, online stages, and intuitive sites give easy to use interfaces, making it simpler for people to take part no matter what their area or earlier logical experience.

Instruction and Effort:

Putting resources into instruction and effort drives is basic for building mindfulness and encouraging a culture of ecological obligation. School programs, local area studios, and public occasions add to natural proficiency and empower dynamic support in resident science.

8. **Contextual analyses:**

BeeSpotter:

BeeSpotter is a resident science project zeroed in on honey bee recognizable proof and checking. Benefactors submit photos of honey bees, supporting specialists in figuring out honey bee populaces, fertilization elements, and the effects of natural changes on these imperative pollinators.

Chile's Public Ranger service Partnership (CONAF) People group Backwoods Observing:

In Chile, CONAF teams up with neighborhood networks to screen and oversee local area backwoods. This people group based approach includes preparing neighborhood occupants to screen backwoods wellbeing, report criminal operations, and effectively take part in supportable woodland the board.

9. **Future Headings and Potential:**

Combination with Customary Biological Information:

The coordination of resident science with conventional natural information upgrades the profundity and lavishness of ecological comprehension. Perceiving and regarding native and neighborhood information frameworks adds to more all encompassing and logically pertinent protection rehearses.

Worldwide Cooperation and Information Sharing:

The potential for worldwide joint effort in resident science is gigantic. Improving information sharing, normalizing conventions, and encouraging worldwide organizations can intensify the effect of resident science on a worldwide scale, tending to transboundary ecological difficulties.

Strategy Reconciliation:

Coordinating resident science into natural strategy making processes improves the importance and relevance of logical examination. State run administrations and organizations can profit from the abundance of information created by resident researchers, integrating this data into preservation and regular asset the board techniques.

4.1Engaging the public in swallow conservation efforts

Swallows, with their elegant flying trapeze artistry and dynamic plumage, are charming birds that assume fundamental parts in keeping up with environmental equilibrium. Sadly, different dangers, from living space misfortune to environmental change, endanger swallow populaces around the world. Connecting with the general population in swallow protection endeavors is basic to shield these avian marvels and their biological systems. This investigation digs into the meaning of swallow preservation, the difficulties looked by these birds, and procedures for preparing public cooperation to guarantee their proceeded with endurance.

1. **The Significance of Swallows in Biological systems:**

   Biological system Administrations:

   Swallows are necessary parts of biological systems, giving significant environment administrations. Their insectivorous eating regimens assist with controlling bug populaces, adding to rural and ranger service bug the board. Swallows assume a pivotal part in keeping up with natural equilibrium by forestalling the unrestrained multiplication of bugs.

   Biodiversity Markers:

   Swallow populaces act as marks of environment wellbeing. Their presence or nonappearance can reflect changes in bug overflow, water quality, and environment conditions. Checking swallow populaces can accordingly offer bits of knowledge into more extensive natural patterns and likely environmental aggravations.

2. **Dangers to Swallow Populaces:**

   Loss of Settling Destinations:

   Urbanization and living space obliteration lead to the deficiency of reasonable settling locales for swallows. The expulsion of mud banks, deforestation, and adjustments to normal scenes deny swallows of urgent settling potential open doors, influencing their conceptive achievement.

   Pesticide Use and Food Source Pollution:

   Swallows' dependence on bugs opens them with the impacts of pesticide use. Horticultural practices that include the broad use of pesticides can sully the bugs swallows consume, influencing their wellbeing and regenerative abilities.

   Environmental Change and Adjusted Movement Examples:

   Environmental change upsets conventional movement examples and modifies the planning of seasons. Swallows, which depend on exact timing for rearing and movement, face difficulties as environment actuated shifts in bug rise and weather conditions influence their capacity to find food and appropriate settling locales.

3. **Connecting with The general population:**

Instructive Projects:

Bringing issues to light about the significance of swallows and the dangers they face is the foundation of public commitment. Instructive projects, school drives, and local area studios can spread data about swallow science, their biological jobs, and the protection challenges they face.

Resident Science Tasks:

Including people in general in logical undertakings through resident science projects cultivates a feeling of pride and obligation. Swallow checking programs, where people contribute perceptions of swallow conduct, settling locales, and populace elements, give significant information to research and preservation endeavors.

Local area Home Box Projects:

Laying out local area home box programs urges nearby occupants to effectively take part in giving appropriate settling destinations to swallows. These drives can include the establishment of swallow-accommodating home boxes in metropolitan and rural regions, making up for the deficiency of normal settling locales.

Territory Rebuilding Occasions:

Local area contribution in territory rebuilding occasions helps address the deficiency of reasonable environments for swallows. Establishing local vegetation, reestablishing wetlands, and making counterfeit mud banks can improve settling open doors and backing swallow populaces.

4. **Instructive Drives:**

School Educational program Incorporation:

Coordinating swallow preservation points into school educational plans improves ecological training and imparts a feeling of natural obligation in people in the future. Curricular modules can cover swallow science, movement designs, and the significance of saving their natural surroundings.

Intelligent Studios and Occasions:

Facilitating intelligent studios and occasions, for example, bird-watching meetings or directed nature strolls, permits people in general to associate straightforwardly with swallows and their living spaces. These encounters make critical associations, encouraging a more profound appreciation for these birds and the requirement for their preservation.

Online Assets and Online classes:

Using on the web stages for instructive assets and online classes expands the span of preservation drives. Enlightening sites, virtual classes, and intelligent online substance make swallow preservation open to a worldwide crowd, empowering different networks to reach out.

5. **Resident Science Undertakings:**

eBird and Swallow Watch:

Incorporating swallow checking into existing resident science stages, like eBird, gives a normalized system to information assortment. Swallow Watch drives can explicitly zero in on observing swallow populaces, settling ways of behaving, and movement designs through cooperative resident science endeavors.

NestWatch and Swallow Home Checking:

NestWatch programs, where residents report settling action of different bird species, can integrate explicit modules for swallow home checking. Members report home areas, egg laying, and fledging, contributing significant information to specialists concentrating on swallow regenerative achievement.

Local area Drove Exploration Activities:

Enabling people group to lead their exploration projects upgrades commitment and considers a more confined comprehension of swallow nature. Local area drove research drives can investigate explicit swallow ways of behaving, neighborhood relocation designs, and the effect of human exercises on swallow populaces.

6. **Local area Home Box Projects:**

Establishment and Support Studios:

Facilitating studios on the establishment and upkeep of swallow home boxes includes the local area straightforwardly in making appropriate natural surroundings. These studios give commonsense abilities and information, empowering people to contribute effectively to swallow protection in their areas.

Embrace a-Home Box Projects:

Carrying out embrace a-home box programs urges local area individuals to get a sense of ownership with explicit home boxes. This customized approach cultivates a feeling of stewardship, as members screen and keep up with the containers, adding to the prosperity of nearby swallow populaces.

Instructive Effort Occasions:

Joining instructive effort occasions with home box programs makes a comprehensive way to deal with public commitment. Occasions can remember exhibitions for home box establishment, educational discussions on swallow biology, and valuable open doors for active association in natural surroundings improvement exercises.

7. **Environment Rebuilding Occasions:**

Local area Establishing Days:

Arranging people group establishing days for local vegetation reclamation adds to making swallow-accommodating natural surroundings. Nearby occupants can partake in establishing meetings, improving green spaces and giving fundamental assets to swallows, like bugs and reasonable settling materials.

Wetland Reclamation Drives:

Swallows frequently depend on wetlands for rummaging and settling. Local area drove wetland reclamation undertakings can include territory cleanup, local plant renewed introduction, and the production of mud banks, tending to basic parts of swallow living space that have been corrupted.

Fake Mud Bank Development:

In metropolitan and rural regions where regular mud banks are scant, networks can team up on building fake mud banks. Studios and occasions zeroed in on building mud banks give both natural surroundings improvement open doors and instructive encounters for members.

8. **Difficulties and Arrangements:**

Absence of Mindfulness:

The absence of mindfulness about swallow protection represents a huge test. Tending to this requires designated instructive missions, local area effort, and joint efforts with schools and nearby associations to scatter data about the significance of swallows.

Restricted Assets:

Restricted assets, both monetary and human, can obstruct the execution of protection drives. Key associations with ecological associations, utilizing local area volunteers, and looking for award potential open doors can assist with defeating asset requirements.

Urbanization and Natural surroundings Misfortune:

Urbanization frequently brings about the deficiency of normal living spaces for swallows. To counter this, local area drove drives ought to zero in on coordinating swallow-accommodating elements into metropolitan scenes, for example, green rooftops, fake mud banks, and home boxes.

9. **Examples of overcoming adversity and Motivations:**

Project MartinRoost:

MartinRoost, a resident science drive, centers around observing swallow perches across North America. By drawing in nearby networks in perch counts, this undertaking has created important information on swallow populaces, adding to a superior comprehension of their way of behaving and dispersion.

The Purple Martin Preservation Affiliation:

The Purple Martin Preservation Affiliation includes networks in the protection of purple martins, a kind of swallow. Through home box programs, instructive drives, and cooperative exploration, this association exhibits the positive effect of local area inclusion on swallow preservation.

4.2 Educating communities about the importance of swallows

Swallows, with their rich airborne showcases and fundamental biological jobs, act as signs of natural wellbeing. Instructing people group about the significance of swallows is essential to gather support for preservation endeavors and encourage a feeling of stewardship towards these avian miracles.

Environmental Equilibrium:

Swallows assume a urgent part in keeping up with environmental equilibrium by controlling bug populaces. Their eating routine fundamentally comprises of flying bugs, including mosquitoes, flies, and horticultural nuisances. By holding bug numbers under control, swallows add to bug the board, guaranteeing the wellbeing of biological systems and farming scenes.

Biodiversity Markers:

Swallows act as marks of biodiversity and environment wellbeing. The presence or nonappearance of swallows can reflect changes in bug overflow and in general biological system conditions. Observing swallow populaces gives significant bits of knowledge into the more extensive natural elements of a district.

Farming Advantages:

Ranchers benefit from the insectivorous idea of swallows. These birds assist with controlling vermin that can harm crops, lessening the requirement for synthetic pesticides. By advancing a characteristic type of vermin the board, swallows add to supportable and harmless to the ecosystem horticultural practices.

Monetary Effect:

Swallows offer financial advantages by supporting agribusiness and decreasing the monetary weight of irritation control. Sound swallow populaces add to flourishing environments, encouraging a sensitive equilibrium that supports biodiversity and supports different ventures subject to stable natural circumstances.

Social Importance:

Swallows hold social importance in numerous social orders, frequently representing best of luck or the appearance of spring. Integrating these social associations into training endeavors cultivates a more profound appreciation for swallows and their part in the embroidery of neighborhood customs and convictions.

Fertilization Help:

While basically insectivorous, some swallow species may coincidentally add to fertilization. Empowering the comprehension of these unpretentious connections adds one more layer to the significance of swallows in keeping up with the complex snare of biological connections.

Worldwide Availability:

Swallows are known for their great relocations, associating far off locales across the globe. Featuring the fantastic excursions of these birds underlines the interconnectedness of environments on a worldwide scale. Their movements highlight the requirement for worldwide collaboration in protection endeavors.

Sign of Natural Change:

Swallows are delicate to ecological changes, making them important signs of movements in environment and territory conditions. Instructing people group about the effect of environmental change on swallow relocation examples and rearing ways of behaving cultivates mindfulness about more extensive ecological issues.

To really instruct networks about the significance of swallows, drives ought to utilize different instructive methodologies. This incorporates studios, instructive materials, intelligent shows, and local area occasions zeroed in on swallow preservation. Connecting with schools, nearby associations, and local area pioneers can enhance the range of instructive projects.

By encouraging a feeling of association among networks and these avian wonders, training turns into an impetus for activity. Enabled people group are bound to help protection drives, carry out swallow-accommodating practices, and effectively partake in territory rebuilding endeavors. Through training, we not just bring issues to light about the meaning of swallows yet in addition move an aggregate obligation to safeguarding these magnetic birds and the biological systems they possess.

4.3 Encouraging citizen science initiatives for monitoring swallow populations

Swallows, with their spry flight designs and crucial environmental jobs, are subjects of expanding worry because of different dangers affecting their populaces. Drawing in networks in resident science drives for checking swallow populaces is a strong technique to assemble important information, bring issues to light, and effectively include the general population in avian preservation endeavors. This complete investigation dives into the meaning of resident science, the job it plays in swallow observing, and methodologies for empowering far and wide cooperation.

1. **Grasping Resident Science:**

Definition and Reason:

Resident science includes including people in general, frequently non-proficient people, in logical exploration. Members, known as resident researchers, add to information assortment, investigation, and perception, extending the degree and size of logical undertakings. With regards to swallow checking, resident science gives a financially savvy and broad method for gathering information on these transient birds.

Advantages of Resident Science:

Resident science offers various advantages, including the preparation of a huge and different labor force, expanded spatial inclusion for information assortment, and the commitment of networks in natural issues. For swallow observing, resident science works with the assortment of information across different locales, empowering specialists to acquire a more complete comprehension of swallow populaces.

2. **The Meaning of Observing Swallow Populaces:**

Environmental Pointers:

Swallows, being insectivorous, are profoundly delicate to changes in bug populaces, making them significant marks of biological wellbeing. Observing swallow populaces permits analysts to survey the wealth of flying bugs, giving bits of knowledge into more extensive biological system elements.

Environmental Change Effect:

Swallows' transitory examples and reproducing ways of behaving are impacted by environment conditions. Observing these examples over the long haul assists scientists with understanding the effect of environmental change on swallow populaces. Changes in relocation timing, settling conduct, or reproducing achievement can give early admonitions of ecological movements.

Preservation Independent direction:

Precise and exceptional data on swallow populaces is fundamental for informed protection independent direction. Resident science information add to the improvement of preservation techniques, living space the executives plans, and strategy proposals to safeguard swallow environments.

3. **Systems for Empowering Resident Science Drives:**

Training and Effort:

1. **Studios and Preparing Projects:**

   Direct studios and preparing projects to teach networks about the significance of swallows and how to take part in resident science drives. These meetings can cover swallow distinguishing proof, information assortment conventions, and the meaning of their job in avian preservation.

2. **Instructive Materials:**

Circulate instructive materials, like leaflets, handouts, and online assets, to furnish members with significant data about swallows, their living spaces, and the objectives of the checking project. Open and drawing in materials can upgrade public comprehension and excitement.

Local area Commitment Occasions:

1. **Bird-Watching Trips:**

   Sort out bird-watching journeys or directed nature strolls zeroed in on swallows. These occasions offer active encounters, permitting members to notice swallows in their regular natural surroundings. Field specialists can give bits of knowledge into swallow conduct and biology.

2. **Public Talks and Talks:**

Have public talks and talks highlighting ornithologists, biologists, or bird specialists. These occasions can feature the significance of swallow checking, share fascinating realities about swallows, and motivate local area individuals to engage in resident science drives.

Innovation Incorporation:

1. **Portable Applications and Online Stages:**

   Influence innovation by creating portable applications or utilizing on the web stages to work with information assortment. Easy to use connection points can urge members to submit perceptions, share photographs, and add to the information base. Stages like eBird have demonstrated fruitful in connecting with resident researchers in bird checking.

2. **Web-based Entertainment Missions:**

Send off web-based entertainment missions to contact a more extensive crowd. Use stages like Facebook, Twitter, and Instagram to share data about swallow checking drives, grandstand member commitments, and make a local area around avian preservation.

Acknowledgment and Impetuses:

1. **Resident Researcher Declarations:**

   Perceive the commitments of resident researchers by giving declarations or affirmations. This proper acknowledgment can impart a deep satisfaction and achievement, propelling members to stay participated in continuous observing endeavors.

2. **Motivation Projects:**

Lay out motivation programs, like awards or little rewards, to empower predictable cooperation. While the characteristic benefit of adding to science is huge, extra motivators can intensify inspiration and support long haul association.

IV. Beating Difficulties:

Information Quality Confirmation:

Execute instructional courses and intensive rules to guarantee information quality. Stress the significance of exact and nitty gritty perceptions, and lay out a framework for confirming and approving resident contributed information.

Local area Inclusivity:

Address boundaries to cooperation by guaranteeing that resident science drives are comprehensive. Think about different socioeconomics, give materials in numerous dialects, and sort out occasions in open areas to draw in a wide range of local area individuals.

Long haul Commitment:

Support commitment by sorting out customary occasions, refreshes, and follow-up exercises. Lay out a feeling of local area among members, cultivating a common obligation to swallow observing that reaches out past one-time commitments.

V. Contextual investigations:

The Cornell Lab of Ornithology - NestWatch:

The NestWatch program, created by the Cornell Lab of Ornithology, connects with resident researchers in checking bird homes, including those of swallows. Members contribute important information on settling achievement, assisting analysts with grasping rearing examples and populace elements.

BirdLife Australia - Swallow Observing Tasks:

BirdLife Australia runs different swallow observing tasks, including people in general in gathering information on swallow species across the landmass. These activities add to public bird data sets and backing designated preservation endeavors for swallow species.

Chapter 5

International Collaboration

In an interconnected world confronting shared difficulties, global cooperation arises as a foundation for resolving complex issues, cultivating common comprehension, and pushing aggregate advancement. From logical examination to discretionary undertakings, coordinated effort among countries assumes an essential part in exploring the intricacies of the 21st 100 years. This investigation digs into the meaning of worldwide cooperation, its different structures across assorted spaces, and the potential it holds for tending to worldwide difficulties.

1. **Grasping Worldwide Coordinated effort:**
   Definition and Degree:
   Global cooperation alludes to the helpful endeavors between nations, associations, or people to address shared objectives and difficulties. This coordinated effort stretches out past boundaries and incorporates an expansive range of fields, including science, innovation, strategy, exchange, natural preservation, and general wellbeing.
   Authentic Development:
   The underlying foundations of global joint effort can be followed back to early human associations, shipping lanes, and social trades. Be that as it may, the idea has advanced altogether in the cutting edge time with the foundation of worldwide associations, arrangements, and arrangements pointed toward advancing harmony, improvement, and collaboration.
2. **Types of Global Coordinated effort:**

Conciliatory and Political Coordinated effort:

1. **Reciprocal Relations:**
   Reciprocal coordinated efforts include collaboration between two nations.

Conciliatory ties, economic accords, and joint drives are normal in two-sided coordinated efforts, advancing common comprehension and shared interests.

2. **Multilateral Associations:**

Multilateral coordinated efforts include various countries and are many times worked with through global associations like the Assembled Countries (UN), World Exchange Association (WTO), and Global Money related Asset (IMF). These associations give stages to countries to by and large resolve worldwide issues.

Logical and Exploration Joint effort:

1. **Joint Exploration Ventures:**

Logical joint effort includes analysts from various nations cooperating on normal examination projects. This works with the pooling of aptitude, assets, and information, prompting headways in different fields, from medication to space investigation.

2. **Worldwide Exploration Foundations:**

Establishments like CERN (European Association for Atomic Exploration), NASA (Public Flight and Space Organization), and the European Space Office embody worldwide coordinated effort in logical undertakings. These associations unite researchers, specialists, and specialists from various countries to investigate the wildernesses of information.

Financial Coordinated effort:

1. **Economic accords:**

Economic accords encourage financial coordinated effort by working with the trading of labor and products between countries. Models incorporate NAFTA (North American International alliance) and the European Association's Single Market.

2. **Global Monetary Foundations:**

Associations like the World Bank and IMF offer monetary help to nations out of luck, advancing financial strength and advancement. These establishments work in light of coordinated effort among part nations.

Ecological and Environment Cooperation:

1. **Environment Arrangements:**

Arrangements, for example, the Paris Understanding unite countries to address environmental change altogether. Through responsibilities and cooperative endeavors, nations expect to diminish ozone harming substance outflows and moderate the effects of an unnatural weather change.

2. **Preservation Drives:**

Cooperative preservation endeavors include numerous countries attempting to safeguard biodiversity, oversee biological systems, and battle ecological corruption. The Show on Organic Variety and global marine preservation arrangements are instances of such drives.

III. The Meaning of Worldwide Cooperation:

Tending to Worldwide Difficulties:

Worldwide coordinated effort is fundamental for handling worldwide difficulties that rise above public lines. Issues, for example, environmental change, pandemics, and psychological warfare require composed endeavors to track down compelling arrangements and moderate their effect on a worldwide scale.

Pooling Assets and Aptitude:

Cooperation empowers the pooling of assets, skill, and innovation. This aggregate methodology upgrades proficiency, speeds up progress, and guarantees that the advantages of headways are divided between taking part countries.

Advancing Harmony and Steadiness:

Cooperative conciliatory endeavors add to the advancement of harmony and security. Exchange and collaboration between countries can assist with forestalling clashes, resolve debates, and encourage a feeling of shared liability regarding worldwide security.

Social Trade and Understanding:

Cooperative drives advance social trade, encouraging shared understanding and appreciation among different social orders. Instructive trades, imaginative coordinated efforts, and joint far-reaching developments add to an additional interconnected and amicable world.

IV. Challenges in Worldwide Coordinated effort:

Political and International Strains:

Political contrasts and international strains can ruin worldwide cooperation. Clashing interests, authentic hatreds, and epic showdowns between countries might hinder joint endeavors to address normal difficulties.

Financial Differences:

Financial differences among countries can make difficulties for joint effort, particularly in monetary and economic deals. Haggling fair terms and guaranteeing comprehensive advantages for all gatherings require sensitive tact and split the difference.

Absence of Trust:

Building trust among countries is vital for fruitful joint effort. Verifiable doubt, worries about information security, and vulnerability about the responsibility of different gatherings can present hindrances to powerful participation.

Social and Phonetic Hindrances:

Social and phonetic contrasts can make correspondence challenges, prompting misconceptions and misinterpretations. Defeating these boundaries expects endeavors to advance social responsiveness and compelling diverse correspondence.

V. Effective Instances of Worldwide Joint effort:

The Human Genome Task:

The Human Genome Task, a global exploration drive, involved researchers from different nations cooperating to guide and grouping the human genome. This co-operative exertion prompted noteworthy progressions in hereditary qualities and medication.

The Worldwide Space Station (ISS):

The ISS is a cooperative undertaking including space organizations from the US, Russia, Europe, Japan, and Canada. This worldwide cooperation has brought about the foundation of a tenable space station for logical examination and investigation.

The Joint Thorough Game plan (JCPOA):

The JCPOA, otherwise called the Iran Atomic Arrangement, is a discretionary understanding including the US, China, Russia, France, Germany, and the European Association. It plans to control Iran's atomic program in return for lifting monetary assents.

The Worldwide Asset to Battle Helps, Tuberculosis, and Jungle fever:

The Worldwide Asset is an organization of legislatures, common society, and the confidential area cooperating to battle Helps, tuberculosis, and jungle fever. This cooperative drive plays had a urgent impact in financing counteraction and treatment programs around the world.

VI. Future Possibilities and Arising Patterns:

Worldwide Wellbeing Joint efforts:

The Coronavirus pandemic has highlighted the significance of worldwide well-being joint efforts. Drives like COVAX, pointed toward guaranteeing evenhanded admittance to Coronavirus immunizations, embody the requirement for aggregate endeavors to address wellbeing emergencies.

Mechanical Advancement Joint efforts:

Joint efforts in arising advancements, like computerized reasoning, biotechnology, and environmentally friendly power, hold the possibility to drive development and address worldwide difficulties. Cross-line organizations in innovative work can prompt extraordinary forward leaps.

Practical Improvement Objectives (SDGs):

The Unified Countries' SDGs give a system to global coordinated effort to re-solve issues, for example, neediness, disparity, environmental change, and natural debasement. Accomplishing these objectives requires facilitated endeavors and associations among countries.

Virtual Cooperation and Advanced Discretion:

Headways in innovation have worked with virtual joint effort and computerized discretion. Online stages, video conferencing, and computerized specialized devices empower countries to team up really without geological limitations.

5.1Importance of cross-border cooperation in swallow conservation

Swallows, with their entrancing ethereal presentations and fundamental environmental jobs, are confronting various dangers that rise above public boundaries. To guarantee the protection and prosperity of these transitory birds, cross-line participation becomes principal. This investigation digs into the significance of cooperative endeavors among countries for swallow preservation, featuring the common obligation in shielding these avian marvels and their natural surroundings.

1. **The Worldwide Meaning of Swallows:**

Transient Examples:

Swallows are eminent for their noteworthy transient excursions that length landmasses. These transitory examples feature the interconnectedness of environments across borders, underlining the requirement for worldwide coordinated effort to safeguard their territories along their whole relocation courses.

Biological Commitments:

Swallows assume critical parts in keeping up with biological equilibrium by controlling bug populaces. Their movement across assorted locales makes them significant supporters of vermin the board in rural scenes, making their protection vital for maintainable and flourishing environments around the world.

2. **Challenges Confronting Swallow Populaces:**

Loss of Natural surroundings:

Urbanization, deforestation, and changes in land use add to the deficiency of pivotal swallow territories. This challenge requires composed endeavors among countries to address living space safeguarding and rebuilding for a bigger scope.

Environmental Change Effects:

Environmental change disturbs customary relocation designs, modifies bug development timings, and impacts atmospheric conditions urgent for swallows. Cooperative techniques are fundamental to comprehend and moderate the impacts of environmental change on swallow populaces internationally.

Pesticide Use:

Swallows' insectivorous eating regimens open them to the effects of pesticide use, which can influence their wellbeing and regenerative achievement.

Worldwide participation is essential to direct and diminish pesticide use in manners that advantage swallow populaces across their assorted territories.

Presentation of Obtrusive Species:

The presentation of obtrusive species presents dangers to swallow settling locales and food sources. Cross-line endeavors are important to forestall and deal with the spread of obtrusive species that adversely influence swallow populaces in different locales.

3. **The Need of Cross-Boundary Participation:**

Transboundary Environments:

Swallows use environments that frequently range numerous nations during their relocation. Collaboration among countries is urgent for the preservation of these transboundary environments, guaranteeing that visit locales, favorable places, and it are enough safeguarded to winter regions.

Relocation Passages:

Distinguishing and saving movement passageways is fundamental for the fruitful relocation of swallows. These halls frequently cross public limits, requiring cooperative drives to address dangers along the whole length of the movement courses.

Information Sharing and Exploration Joint effort:

Cooperative examination endeavors empower the sharing of significant information on swallow populaces, ways of behaving, and natural circumstances. Worldwide collaboration in research drives upgrades the comprehension of worldwide swallow elements, illuminating protection techniques.

Strategy Arrangement:

Fitting preservation arrangements among adjoining nations is essential. Predictable guidelines with respect to territory security, pesticide use, and natural administration add to a brought together methodology that advantages swallow populaces across borders.

4. **Contextual analyses in Cross-Boundary Swallow Preservation:**

EuroBirdPortal:

EuroBirdPortal is a cooperative stage that accumulates and shares bird relocation information across Europe. This drive permits taking part nations to contribute and get to data about bird developments, including those of swallows, cultivating cross-line collaboration in observing and research.

The East Asian-Australasian Flyway Organization (EAAFP):

The EAAFP is a joint effort among nations across East Asia and Australasia to moderate transitory waterbirds, including some swallow species. Through joint protection activities and drives, countries cooperate to shield basic environments along the flyway.

African-Eurasian Transient Landbirds Activity Plan (AEMLAP):

AEMLAP is a cooperative exertion including African and Eurasian nations to address the protection challenges looked by transitory landbirds, including swallows. This activity plan intends to improve global collaboration for the security of basic living spaces and relocation courses.

5. **Methodologies for Powerful Cross-Line Participation:**

Foundation of Protection Organizations:

Making transnational organizations and associations committed to swallow protection cultivates joint effort. These organizations work with data trade, joint drives, and composed activities among nations.

Shared Exploration Drives:

Cooperative examination projects empower researchers and progressives from various countries to cooperate. Shared drives can zero in on following relocation designs, concentrating on environment inclinations, and recognizing dangers that require joint relief systems.

Strategy Harmonization:

Adjusting preservation strategies among adjoining nations guarantees a brought together front in safeguarding swallows. Shared guidelines with respect to living space safeguarding, supportable land use, and pesticide the executives add to powerful cross-line protection.

Local area Commitment Across Boundaries:

Connecting with nearby networks in preservation endeavors is essential, and this commitment ought to reach out across borders. Instructive projects, local area drove drives, and living space rebuilding undertakings can include occupants from adjoining nations, advancing a feeling of shared liability.

6. **Challenges in Cross-Boundary Joint effort:**

Varying Needs and Assets:

Nations might have changing protection needs and accessible assets. Accomplishing agreement on shared objectives and tending to asset incongruities requires conciliatory talks and a pledge to evenhanded joint effort.

Political and International Strains:

Political contrasts and international strains can convolute cross-line joint effort. Open correspondence, conciliatory endeavors, and stressing shared natural interests can assist with defeating political difficulties.

Information Sharing and Protection Concerns:

Sharing biological information across boundaries might raise worries about protection and information security. Laying out conventions for dependable information sharing, while at the same time regarding protection concerns, is vital for effective coordinated effort.

Social and Etymological Contrasts:

Social and etymological incongruities can influence correspondence and understanding. Endeavors to connect these holes through social trade programs and multilingual coordinated efforts can upgrade cross-line collaboration.

7. **Advantages and Future Possibilities:**

Biodiversity Preservation:

Cross-line coordinated effort adds to the protection of biodiversity past public limits. Safeguarding swallow populaces in their whole reach guarantees the protection of different biological systems and the species that occupy them.

Improved Versatility:

Cooperative endeavors make swallow populaces stronger to natural difficulties. By tending to dangers completely and sharing accepted procedures, nations add to the general flexibility of these transitory birds.

Logical Headways:

Global joint effort cultivates logical headways in swallow research. Joint endeavors empower the improvement of inventive preservation procedures, mechanical arrangements, and a more profound comprehension of swallow ways of behaving and needs.

Worldwide Ecological Administration:

Fruitful cross-line participation in swallow preservation starts a trend for compelling worldwide natural administration. It lays out a system for tending to other transboundary preservation challenges and supports the idea that ecological stewardship is a common obligation.

5.2 Sharing success stories and best practices globally

In the domain of swallow protection, the scattering of examples of overcoming adversity and best practices on a worldwide scale fills in as a strong impetus for positive change. Sharing encounters and examples learned motivates preservation endeavors as well as cultivates cooperation, empowering countries to pursue the insurance of these avian ponders aggregately. This concise investigation dives into the significance of sharing examples of overcoming adversity and best practices with regards to swallow protection.

Motivation for Protection Activity:

Examples of overcoming adversity in swallow preservation act as signals of motivation for people, networks, and countries. Featuring cases where deliberate endeavors have prompted the recuperation or flourishing of swallow populaces ingrains a feeling of trust and assurance. Examples of overcoming adversity feature that proactive preservation measures can yield positive results, propelling others to start comparable endeavors.

Gaining from Best Practices:

Best practices embody the best and manageable ways to deal with swallow preservation. Sharing these practices universally gives an abundance of information that can be adjusted and carried out across different environments and locales. Whether it's effective territory reclamation, inventive local area commitment systems, or significant strategy executions, best practices offer a guide for different countries confronting comparative preservation challenges.

Advancing Joint effort:

The worldwide dividing of examples of overcoming adversity and best practices works with joint effort between countries. By understanding what has functioned admirably in various settings, nations can shape cooperative organizations, share assets, and altogether address transboundary preservation issues. Such cooperation cultivates a feeling of shared liability and a brought together front in shielding swallow populaces.

Engaging Nearby People group:

Examples of overcoming adversity frequently spotlight the dynamic association of nearby networks in preservation endeavors. By sharing these stories universally, networks overall can find out about successful ways of drawing in with and enable neighborhood occupants. Effective people group drove drives, whether in making swallow-accommodating territories or bringing issues to light, become significant layouts for others endeavoring to include their networks in protection.

Fortifying Preservation Strategies:

States can draw bits of knowledge from examples of overcoming adversity and best practices to upgrade their protection strategies. Instances of fruitful approach executions, for example, environment security measures or guidelines on pesticide use, offer direction for creating compelling and reasonable preservation structures. This trade of information adds to the advancement of hearty and versatile preservation arrangements all around the world.

Contextual investigations as Instructive Apparatuses:

Examples of overcoming adversity and best practices act as unmistakable contextual investigations for instructive purposes. Integrating these certifiable models into instructive educational plans, preparing projects, and effort drives teaches general society, understudies, and experts about the complexities of swallow preservation. Gaining from genuine encounters cultivates a more profound comprehension of the difficulties confronted and the arrangements carried out.

Worldwide Protection Stages:

Worldwide gatherings and stages committed to preservation, like meetings, studios, and online data sets, give roads to the worldwide sharing of examples of overcoming adversity and best practices. These stages make spaces for specialists, moderates, and policymakers to trade information, talk about difficulties, and altogether plan for the fate of swallow protection.

5.3 Advocating for policies that support swallow conservation on a global scale

Swallows, with their agile flight and natural importance, face various dangers that require extensive and composed preservation endeavors. Upholding for strategies on a worldwide scale is significant to address the intricate difficulties facing swallow populaces. This investigation dives into the significance of pushing for arrangements that help swallow preservation, underscoring the requirement for global cooperation to guarantee the security of these transitory birds.

1. **Figuring out the Worldwide Extent of Swallow Protection:**

   Transboundary Relocation:

   Swallows leave on cross-country travels, navigating lines and biological systems. To actually preserve these birds, approaches should think about the whole transitory courses, spreading over rearing, settling, and wintering regions, and include various nations in facilitated endeavors.

   Shared Biological systems:

   Swallows possess assorted environments that frequently cross-over across countries. Strategies should perceive the interconnectedness of these environments and address issues, for example, living space misfortune, environmental change, and pesticide utilize that stretch out past individual lines.

2. **Significance of Worldwide Approaches:**

   Reliable Preservation Norms:

   Worldwide approaches lay out steady norms for swallow protection. Normal rules guarantee that countries take on bound together methodologies, forestalling variations in preservation endeavors and elevating an orchestrated reaction to shared difficulties.

   Relieving Anthropogenic Dangers:

   Anthropogenic dangers, including living space annihilation, pesticide use, and environmental change, require cooperative arrangements. Worldwide strategies can address these dangers altogether, integrating best practices and logical experiences to alleviate their effect on swallow populaces.

   Safeguarding Biodiversity:

   Swallows add to biodiversity by controlling bug populaces and filling in as marks of biological system wellbeing. Worldwide approaches pointed toward protecting biodiversity perceive the interconnectedness of species and environments, recognizing the significance of swallows in keeping up with natural equilibrium.

3. **Parts of Worldwide Support:**

   Logical Exploration and Information Sharing:

   Support for worldwide arrangements requires powerful logical examination and information sharing. Cooperative investigations on swallow conduct, movement examples, and populace elements add to the detailing of proof based strategies that address the particular necessities of these birds.

   Natural surroundings Assurance and Rebuilding:

   Strategies ought to accentuate environment insurance and reclamation on a global scale. Distinguishing and protecting basic living spaces, including rearing and transient visit destinations, is fundamental for the drawn out preservation of swallow populaces.

Controlling Pesticide Use:

Promotion endeavors ought to zero in on worldwide arrangements directing pesticide use. Composed ways to deal with decrease hurtful synthetic compounds, advance reasonable cultivating rehearses, and safeguard bug populaces line up with the preservation needs of insectivorous swallows.

Environmental Change Alleviation:

Worldwide approaches addressing environmental change are essential to swallow preservation. Support ought to advance peaceful accords that mean to decrease ozone depleting substance outflows, alleviate environment related effects, and protect the living spaces urgent for swallow endurance.

4. **The Job of Global Associations:**

Joined Countries System:

The Assembled Countries (UN) gives a stage to worldwide coordinated effort on natural issues. Promotion endeavors can use UN systems, like the Show on Natural Variety, to accentuate the significance of swallow preservation and encourage worldwide participation.

Territorial Natural Arrangements:

Territorial natural arrangements, like those inside the European Association or ASEAN, assume a fundamental part in forming strategies. Promoters can work inside these systems to adjust territorial strategies to worldwide preservation objectives for swallows.

5. **Promotion Methodologies:**

Raise Worldwide Mindfulness:

Support starts with raising worldwide mindfulness about the situation of swallows. Using online entertainment, instructive missions, and worldwide occasions helps accumulate support and urges countries to focus on swallow preservation in their approaches.

Connect with Partners:

Connecting with partners, including legislatures, NGOs, researchers, and nearby networks, is critical. Building collusions and alliances across borders reinforce support endeavors and make an aggregate voice for swallow protection on the worldwide stage.

Strategy Proposals:

Foster clear and significant arrangement suggestions informed by logical examination and preservation skill. These suggestions ought to address the particular difficulties looked by swallows and propose arrangements that line up with worldwide protection targets.

Entryway for Global Coordinated effort:

Advocate for expanded global joint effort through strategic channels, empowering countries to cooperate in creating and executing arrangements that help swallow protection. Underline the common obligation in safeguarding these transient birds.

6. **Examples of overcoming adversity and Best Practices:**

Exhibiting Successful Strategies:

Featuring examples of overcoming adversity where viable strategies have emphatically influenced swallow populaces is a strong backing instrument. Sharing accepted procedures universally gives substantial instances of how countries can add to swallow preservation through insightful approaches.

Exhibiting Financial and Environmental Advantages:

Promotion endeavors ought to accentuate the monetary and environmental advantages of swallow protection. Solid swallow populaces add to bug control, support agrarian practices, and upgrade generally biological system strength, highlighting the significance of approaches that defend these avian partners.

Chapter 6

Future Challenges And Opportunities

As we look toward the eventual fate of swallow protection, an embroidery of difficulties and potential open doors unfurls. Swallows, with their complicated transitory examples and biological importance, face a powerful scene molded by human exercises, ecological changes, and worldwide interconnectedness. This investigation dives into the forthcoming difficulties that might affect swallow populaces and the valuable open doors that exist in our grip to guarantee their supported presence on our planet.

1. **Future Difficulties in Swallow Preservation:**

   Environmental Change Elements:

   Changed Movement Examples and Rearing Ways of behaving

   Environmental change keeps on reshaping biological systems, influencing the accessibility of food sources and modifying weather conditions urgent for swallow movement. Swallows, finely receptive to natural signals, may confront difficulties in adjusting their relocation courses and rearing ways of behaving, affecting their generally speaking conceptive achievement.

   Environment Versatile Protection Methodologies

   Creating environment versatile protection methodologies is basic. This includes checking and understanding the developing effects of environmental change on swallows, adjusting protection designs likewise, and making territories that can endure changing ecological circumstances.

   Environment Discontinuity and Urbanization:

   Loss of Basic Living spaces

   Quick urbanization and natural surroundings discontinuity present huge difficulties for swallows. The deficiency of regular settling locales, disturbed scrounging grounds, and expanded openness to metropolitan risks can impede the birds' capacity to track down reasonable natural surroundings, affecting their rearing and transitory achievement.

Natural surroundings Conservation and Reclamation Drives

Putting resources into environment safeguarding and reclamation drives is significant. Establishing and keeping up with swallow-accommodating conditions, even in metropolitan regions, through green spaces, fake settling designs, and preservation agreeable metropolitan arranging can moderate the effects of territory misfortune.

Pesticide Use and Agrarian Practices:

Effect on Bug Populaces

Serious pesticide use in horticulture represents a danger to swallow populaces by lessening the overflow of flying bugs, an essential food hotspot for these birds. Lessened bug populaces can prompt nourishing lacks for swallows, influencing their wellbeing and regenerative abilities.

Advancing Feasible Cultivating Practices

Supporting for and carrying out maintainable cultivating practices can relieve the antagonistic impacts of pesticides. Incorporated bother the executives, natural cultivating, and agroecological approaches advance biodiversity, giving swallows a more than adequate stock of bugs while keeping up with farming efficiency.

Intrusive Species and Contest for Assets:

Disturbance of Biological system Equilibrium

The presentation of intrusive species can upset environments, prompting expanded rivalry for assets among bird species, including swallows. Obtrusive species may outcompete local birds for settling destinations and food sources, adversely influencing swallow populaces.

Intrusive Species The board Techniques

Executing successful obtrusive species the board techniques is imperative. This incorporates early identification and annihilation endeavors, natural reclamation to upgrade local biodiversity, and research to comprehend and address the environmental effects of intrusive species on swallows.

Worldwide Pandemics and Sickness Flare-ups:

Arising Wellbeing Dangers

The event of worldwide pandemics and infection flare-ups represents a likely danger to swallow populaces. Illnesses influencing the two people and natural life, like avian flu, can have flowing consequences for environments, affecting the wellbeing and endurance of swallow populaces.

Checking and Readiness

Putting resources into checking projects to follow the soundness of swallow populaces and being ready for illness episodes is significant. Early location, investigation into sickness transmission elements, and carrying out measures to forestall the spread of illnesses can assist with moderating the effect on swallows.

2. **Future Open doors in Swallow Protection:**

Progressions in Innovation:

Mechanical Answers for Observing and Exploration

Quick headways in innovation offer extraordinary open doors for swallow protection. Satellite following, drones, and bioacoustic observing give imaginative instruments to following relocation designs, examining settling ways of behaving, and acquiring bits of knowledge into swallow nature.

Resident Science and Publicly supported Information

Connecting with the general population in checking endeavors through resident science drives, portable applications, and online stages outfits the force of publicly supported information. This cooperative methodology improves information assortment, gives ongoing data, and cultivates a feeling of shared liability regarding swallow protection.

Worldwide Network and Joint effort:

Worldwide Participation for Protection

Our universally associated world offers an exceptional chance for cooperative protection endeavors. Worldwide associations, information trade, and composed activities among countries can address transboundary challenges and advance the preservation of swallow populaces across their immense transient reaches.

Diverse Schooling and Mindfulness

Using worldwide availability for diverse schooling and mindfulness can upgrade understanding and backing for swallow protection. Tackling computerized stages, online entertainment, and virtual commitment drives can make a worldwide local area committed to the prosperity of these transient birds.

Public Mindfulness and Ecological Instruction:

Building a Preservation Ethic

Elevating public mindfulness and cultivating ecological schooling are significant open doors for swallow preservation. Teaching people group about the significance of swallows, their natural jobs, and the dangers they face can impart a protection ethic, prompting educated and proactive stewardship.

Promotion for Strategy Changes

A very much educated public can act as backers for strategy changes. Engaged people group can voice their interests, campaign for more grounded protection strategies, and consider legislatures responsible for economical practices that advantage swallow populaces and the more extensive environment.

Protection Financing and Magnanimity:

Assembling Assets for Protection

The rising familiarity with ecological difficulties has prompted a flood in protection subsidizing and magnanimity. Utilizing these assets for swallow protection drives, research ventures, and living space rebuilding projects can fundamentally add to the prosperity of these avian species.

Corporate and NGO Organizations

Joint effort between companies, non-legislative associations (NGOs), and protection elements presents a chance to pool assets and mastery. Corporate sponsorships, charitable organizations, and joint drives can drive significant protection projects for a bigger scope.

Strategy Backing and Official Help:

Worldwide Approach Promotion for Swallow Protection

Upholding for worldwide strategies that help swallow protection is a critical open door. Drawing in with policymakers, impacting peaceful accords, and adjusting preservation objectives to more extensive ecological strategies can establish a favorable administrative climate for swallow security.

Lawful Insurances and Preservation Motivations

Legislatures can assume an essential part in giving lawful securities and protection impetuses. Carrying out regulations that defend swallow living spaces, control unsafe practices, and give motivations to protection endeavors can make a steady structure for long haul preservation achievement.

6.1 Anticipating emerging threats to swallow populations

The world is continually developing, driven by innovative headways, cultural changes, and worldwide interconnectedness. As we stand at the slope representing things to come, a bunch of difficulties and open doors look for us. This powerful scene requests a proactive and versatile way to deal with explore the intricacies that lie ahead. In this investigation, we will dig into the vital future difficulties and open doors that will shape our reality.

1. **Innovative Insurgency:**

1. **Man-made reasoning and Computerization:**

    The ascent of man-made reasoning (computer based intelligence) and mechanization presents the two difficulties and open doors. On one hand, these advances can possibly alter ventures, smooth out cycles, and upgrade effectiveness. In any case, worries about work uprooting and moral ramifications of computer based intelligence frameworks pose a potential threat. Finding some kind of harmony between mechanical development and moral contemplations will be critical in saddling the maximum capacity of simulated intelligence.

2. **Network protection Dangers:**

As innovation propels, so do the dangers in the computerized domain. Network safety challenges have become more modern, compromising individual protection as well as public safety. Reinforcing network safety measures, encouraging global coordinated effort, and creating strong frameworks will be basic to shielding our undeniably interconnected world.

II. Ecological Supportability:

1. Environmental Change:

The major problem of environmental change stays a critical test. Climbing temperatures, outrageous climate occasions, and natural corruption represent a danger to environments and human prosperity. Alleviating environmental change requires deliberate worldwide endeavors, including the reception of maintainable practices, sustainable power sources, and peaceful accords.

2. Asset Shortage:

Developing populaces and expanded utilization strain Earth's limited assets. The consumption of water, energy, and natural substances presents difficulties for manageable turn of events. Embracing round economy standards, putting resources into inexhaustible assets, and advancing capable utilization are fundamental for tending to asset shortage.

III. Social and Segment Movements:

1. Maturing Populace:

Numerous social orders are encountering a segment shift with a maturing populace. While expanded future is a demonstration of clinical headways, it brings difficulties, for example, medical services loads, benefits manageability, and changes in labor markets. Developments in medical care, social approaches, and intergenerational joint effort will be significant in tending to the ramifications of a maturing populace.

2. Urbanization and Megacities:

Fast urbanization is changing the worldwide scene. The development of megacities achieves foundation challenges, expanded interest for assets, and social inconsistencies. Metropolitan arranging that focuses on manageability, savvy innovations, and evenhanded improvement is fundamental for making decent and strong urban communities.

IV. Worldwide Wellbeing:

1. Pandemic Readiness:

The Coronavirus pandemic has highlighted the significance of worldwide wellbeing readiness. Future difficulties might incorporate arising irresistible sicknesses, anti-infection obstruction, and wellbeing inconsistencies. Reinforcing medical care frameworks, putting resources into innovative work, and encouraging global participation are basic for overseeing future wellbeing emergencies.

2. **Psychological well-being Mindfulness:**

As cultural assumptions advance, psychological well-being issues are earning respect. Stress, uneasiness, and despondency are common difficulties that influence people across socioeconomics. Destigmatizing emotional wellness, advancing mindfulness, and incorporating emotional wellness support into medical care frameworks are amazing chances to improve by and large prosperity.

V. Financial Change:

1. **Pay Disparity:**
   Monetary inconsistencies persevere all around the world, presenting difficulties to social attachment and steadiness. Tending to pay disparity requires a complex methodology, including moderate tax collection, social security nets, and comprehensive monetary strategies that advance equivalent open doors.

2. **Fourth Modern Unrest:**

The continuous Fourth Modern Unrest, portrayed by the combination of computerized, organic, and actual advances, offers exceptional open doors for development and monetary development. Notwithstanding, guaranteeing that the advantages are shared evenhandedly and that the labor force is ready for the changing position scene is essential.

VI. Training and Long lasting Learning:

1. **Innovation in Training:**
   Progressions in innovation are reshaping training, offering better approaches for mastering and expertise advancement. Incorporating innovation into instruction can improve access, customized learning, and worldwide joint effort. Be that as it may, guaranteeing advanced proficiency, tending to the computerized partition, and reconsidering instruction models are fundamental for saddling these open doors.

2. **Deep rooted Learning:**

The quickly developing position market requires a shift towards long lasting learning. Consistent expertise improvement and flexibility will be critical for people to flourish in an evolving labor force. States, organizations, and instructive establishments should team up to make a culture of deep rooted learning and give available open doors to upskilling and reskilling.

6.2 Identifying research gaps and the need for further studies

Research is a powerful cycle that adds to the development of information in different fields. Notwithstanding, any collection of information will undoubtedly have holes and unanswered inquiries. Perceiving and tending to these holes is basic for the progression of understanding and the improvement of viable applications. Here, we dig into the significance of distinguishing research holes and the convincing requirement for additional examinations.

Improving Information Continuum:

Recognizing research holes fills in as the impetus for the persistent advancement of information. It recognizes that how we might interpret a subject is a dynamic and progressing process. By pinpointing regions where data is missing or clashing, scientists can propose new inquiries and roads for investigation, subsequently guaranteeing the information continuum stays whole.

Refining Techniques and Approaches:

Research holes frequently demonstrate regions where flow philosophies or approaches might miss the mark. Perceiving these weaknesses permits analysts to refine existing techniques or foster creative methodologies. This iterative course of refinement not just adds to the exactness and unwavering quality of exploration results yet additionally makes ready for additional successful procedures later on.

Illuminating Arrangement and Practice:

Recognizing research holes has significant ramifications for this present reality uses of information. Policymakers, specialists, and industry experts depend on research discoveries to pursue informed choices. Tending to explore holes guarantees that these partners approach thorough and modern data, in this way impacting strategy plan and functional applications in a way that lines up with the present status of information.

Advancing Interdisciplinary Coordinated effort:

Research holes frequently rise above disciplinary limits, requiring cooperative endeavors from assorted fields. Recognizing these holes energizes interdisciplinary cooperation, uniting specialists with shifted viewpoints and philosophies. Such coordinated efforts enhance the examination interaction as well as cultivate comprehensive answers for complex issues that may not be enough tended to inside a solitary discipline.

Directing Future Exploration Plans:

Research holes act as guideposts for setting future examination plans. By understanding what stays obscure or deficiently investigated, specialists can adjust their endeavors to the most squeezing and significant inquiries. This essential center guarantees that assets are coordinated toward regions that can possibly make critical commitments to the headway of information.

6.3Exploring innovative technologies and approaches for conservation

Protection, despite remarkable ecological difficulties, is developing through the reconciliation of inventive advances and novel methodologies. The customary strategies for saving biodiversity and biological systems are demonstrating deficient right after environmental change, territory misfortune, and human exercises. In this investigation, we will dive into the astonishing universe of creative advances and approaches that are reshaping the scene of preservation, offering new expectation for the security of our planet's valuable normal assets.

1. **Innovation in Natural life Observing:**

1. **Satellite Innovation:**

   Satellite innovation has altered untamed life observing and preservation endeavors. High-goal satellite symbolism empowers specialists to screen changes in living space, track creature developments, and recognize expected dangers to biodiversity. This innovation works with a complete comprehension of huge scope biological systems, supporting the detailing of successful preservation techniques.

2. **GPS Following and Telemetry:**

   Progresses in GPS following and telemetry gadgets have considered exact following of individual creatures. Scientists can screen relocation designs, natural surroundings use, and conduct progressively. This data is significant for planning safeguarded regions, grasping species communications, and alleviating human-natural life clashes.

3. **Camera Traps and Sensor Organizations:**

   Camera traps outfitted with movement sensors have turned into a staple in untamed life research. These inconspicuous gadgets catch pictures and recordings of subtle species, giving bits of knowledge into populace elements and conduct. Combined with sensor organizations, these devices offer a financially savvy and painless method for checking biodiversity in remote or testing landscapes.

II. Protection Hereditary qualities and Biotechnology:

1. **Genomic Approaches:**

   Protection hereditary qualities influences genomic advances to evaluate hereditary variety inside populaces. Understanding hereditary fluctuation is urgent for the drawn out endurance of species, particularly those confronting little populace sizes. Genomic devices help in recognizing people for rearing projects, moderating inbreeding, and safeguarding versatile characteristics.

2. **CRISPR and Hereditary Salvage:**

The progressive CRISPR innovation can possibly resolve hereditary issues in jeopardized species. Hereditary salvage includes acquainting gainful attributes into populaces with improve their wellness and versatility. While moral contemplations flourish, CRISPR offers a device for designated mediations in protection science.

III. Man-made reasoning and Information Examination:

1. **AI for Protection Arranging:**

   AI calculations process immense datasets to recognize examples and relationships. In preservation arranging, these apparatuses help with foreseeing species dissemination, evaluating environment appropriateness, and distinguishing regions in danger. AI improves the productivity and accuracy of preservation endeavors.

2. **Prescient Investigation for Poaching Anticipation:**

Prescient examination, joined with constant information, can be an incredible asset in forestalling poaching. By dissecting verifiable poaching occurrences, weather conditions, and creature developments, prescient models can assist specialists with designating assets decisively to hinder criminal operations.

IV. Resident Science and Local area Commitment:

1. **Versatile Applications for Information Assortment:**

   Versatile applications engage resident researchers to contribute important information for preservation research. From recognizing species to detailing ecological changes, these applications connect with general society in logical undertakings, cultivating a feeling of pride and obligation towards nearby environments.

2. **Local area Based Protection:**

Including neighborhood networks in protection endeavors is basic for long haul achievement. Local area based protection approaches think about native information, include networks in direction, and address financial variables adding to natural debasement.

V. Environmental Change Relief and Transformation:

1. **Bioengineering and Carbon Catch:**

   Bioengineering arrangements, like afforestation and reforestation, add to carbon catch and capacity. Creative methodologies, including the improvement of carbon-retaining materials and advancements, assume a part in relieving the effects of environmental change on biodiversity.

2. **Environment Tough Preservation Systems:**

Protection endeavors need to adjust to changing climatic circumstances. Carrying out environment strong techniques includes distinguishing and safeguarding refugia, planning passages for species relocation, and elevating biological system rebuilding to improve by and large flexibility.

VI. Challenges and Moral Contemplations:

1. **Protection Concerns and Information Security:**

   The utilization of cutting edge innovations raises worries about protection, particularly with regards to observing human-natural life associations. Finding some kind of harmony between information assortment for preservation and regarding individual protection is a urgent moral thought.

2. **Impartial Access and Inclusivity:**

   The reception of imaginative advancements ought to be comprehensive, guaranteeing that networks, especially those in asset restricted regions, have evenhanded access. This advances a more complete comprehension of environments and forestalls the prohibition of imperative viewpoints.

3. **Moral Contemplations in Hereditary Mediations:**

The utilization of biotechnological devices like CRISPR in protection raises moral problems. Inquiries regarding the purposeful change of genomes, expected potentially negative results, and the drawn out natural effects require cautious thought and moral systems.

Chapter 7

Educational Programs And Outreach

Instructive projects and effort drives assume a urgent part in molding the future by giving information, abilities, and open doors for people and networks. These undertakings span holes in admittance to schooling, encourage inclusivity, and engage individuals to understand their maximum capacity. In this exhaustive investigation, we dig into the different scene of instructive projects and effort, looking at their importance, influence, and the developing methodologies that drive positive change.

1. **Admittance to Schooling: Breaking Boundaries and Encouraging Inclusivity**
   1. **Worldwide Instructive Inconsistencies:**
      Instructive projects and effort drives address worldwide variations in admittance to quality schooling. While certain areas benefit from deeply grounded schooling systems, others face difficulties like inadequate framework, absence of assets, and social obstructions. Outreach programs intend to separate these obstructions, guaranteeing that schooling turns into an all inclusive right.
   2. **Orientation Uniformity in Schooling:**

Accomplishing orientation uniformity in schooling stays a basic objective. Instructive projects and effort endeavors center around wiping out orientation based segregation, giving equivalent open doors to young men and young ladies. Drives that challenge generalizations, advance female initiative in schooling, and address social predispositions add to encouraging a more comprehensive learning climate.

II. Youth Instruction: Establishing the Groundwork for Long lasting Learning

1. **Significance of Youth Instruction:**

   Youth instruction frames the bedrock of a youngster's mental, close to home, and social turn of events. Instructive projects focusing on youth intend to give an invigorating climate that sustains interest and establishes the groundwork for a deep rooted love of learning. The effect of early instruction stretches out past scholastic accomplishments, impacting in general prosperity.

2. **Local area Based Early Learning Habitats:**

Local area based early learning places carry schooling to the doorstep of underserved networks. These focuses offer scholarly help as well as deal a safe and supporting space for youngsters. Cooperative endeavors including instructors, guardians, and nearby networks are critical to the outcome of such drives.

III. STEM Schooling: Cultivating Advancement and Decisive Reasoning

1. **The Job of STEM in Schooling:**

   Science, innovation, designing, and math (STEM) schooling is instrumental in planning people for the difficulties of a quickly propelling world. Instructive projects in STEM fields underscore decisive reasoning, critical thinking, and imagination. Drives elevating STEM training add to the improvement of a talented labor force and drive development.

2. **Young ladies in STEM: Tending to Orientation Abberations:**

Regardless of progress, orientation variations persevere in STEM fields. Outreach programs focusing on young ladies in STEM expect to challenge generalizations, give mentorship, and establish comprehensive learning conditions. Empowering young ladies to seek after STEM instruction improves variety as well as takes advantage of a more extensive pool of ability.

IV. Computerized Education and Innovation Driven Learning

1. **Computerized Separation and Comprehensive Innovation Schooling:**

   The computerized partition represents a critical test to impartial schooling. Instructive projects addressing computerized proficiency and giving admittance to innovation overcome this issue. Comprehensive innovation training guarantees that people, no matter what their financial foundation, can saddle the force of advanced apparatuses for learning.

2. **E-Learning Stages and Mixed Learning:**

The rise of e-learning stages and mixed learning models reforms conventional training. Instructive projects utilizing these stages offer adaptability, customized growth opportunities, and valuable open doors for ability improvement. Mixed learning consolidates on the web and disconnected assets, taking care of assorted learning styles.

V. Professional Preparation and Expertise Improvement: Enabling for What's in store

1. **Changing Scene of Work:**

   The idea of work is developing, with a developing accentuation on ranges of abilities lined up with innovative headways. Professional preparation and expertise improvement programs overcome any issues between customary schooling and the abilities requested by the gig market. These projects enable people to effectively explore the changing scene of work.

2. **Business Instruction: Encouraging Development and Drive:**

Business instruction ingrains a feeling of development, innovativeness, and drive. Outreach drives supporting business instruction furnish hopeful business people with the information and abilities expected to begin and support fruitful endeavors. Cultivating an innovative outlook adds to financial development and local area advancement.

VI. Local area Commitment and Partner Cooperation

1. **The Job of Networks in Schooling:**

   Local area commitment is integral to the progress of instructive projects. Drives that include neighborhood networks in direction, educational program improvement, and execution make a feeling of pride and importance. Cooperative endeavors between instructive foundations, guardians, and local area pioneers reinforce the general effect of training.

2. **Corporate Social Obligation in Schooling:**

Corporate substances assume a critical part in supporting schooling through corporate social obligation (CSR) drives. These projects might incorporate financing instructive ventures, giving assets, or offering mentorship open doors. Joint effort among organizations and instructive establishments adds to comprehensive local area advancement.

VII. Ecological Training: Cultivating Stewardship and Manageability

1. **Significance of Ecological Schooling:**

   Notwithstanding ecological difficulties, training turns into an integral asset for cultivating natural stewardship and manageability. Instructive projects fixated on ecological mindfulness ingrain a feeling of obligation towards the planet, advancing reasonable practices and protection endeavors.

2. Open air and Experiential Learning:

Open air and experiential learning programs give involved encounters that extend understanding and appreciation for the climate. Whether through nature-based exercises, eco-accommodating ventures, or field trips, these drives interface students with the normal world and ingrain a feeling of ecological obligation.

VIII. Difficulties and Future Contemplations

1. Tending to Imbalance in Access:

Notwithstanding progress, disparity in admittance to schooling endures. Conquering this challenge requires resolving fundamental issues, supporting for strategy changes, and guaranteeing that instructive projects are planned in light of inclusivity.

2. Adjusting to Mechanical Changes:

The fast speed of mechanical change presents the two potential open doors and difficulties. Instructive projects should adjust to arising advances, guaranteeing that students are furnished with the abilities required for the future work market.

3. Worldwide Coordinated effort for Reasonable Effect:

Worldwide difficulties require worldwide arrangements. Cooperative endeavors between countries, associations, and networks can enhance the effect of instructive projects, encouraging manageable turn of events and positive cultural change.

7.1 Developing educational materials for schools and communities

Creating compelling instructive materials is a foundation in the undertaking to make open and significant growth opportunities for people inside schools and networks. Fitting assets to different necessities, cultivating commitment, and guaranteeing pertinence are vital parts of this cycle. In this investigation, we dig into the meaning of making instructive materials, the standards directing their turn of events, and the extraordinary effect they can have on learning conditions.

1. The Significance of Instructive Materials: An Impetus for Learning

1. Improving Admittance to Quality Schooling:

Instructive materials assume a significant part in democratizing admittance to quality schooling. They span holes in assets and give a normalized establishment to picking up, guaranteeing that understudies, no matter what their experiences, have equivalent chances to gain information.

2. Supporting Different Learning Styles:

People have different learning styles and inclinations. Instructive materials can be custom fitted to oblige these distinctions, integrating visual guides, intuitive components, and shifted organizations to speak to various sorts of students. This inclusivity encourages a more successful and drawing in growth opportunity.

II. Standards of Powerful Instructive Material Turn of events:

1. **Grasping the Main interest group:**

   Fitting instructive materials requires a profound comprehension of the interest group. Whether planning for explicit grade levels, social settings, or abilities to learn, designers should consider the interesting requirements and attributes of the students who will connect with the materials.

2. **Lining up with Educational program Guidelines:**

   Instructive materials should line up with educational program guidelines to guarantee importance and consistency with instructive objectives. Planning content to laid out systems upgrades the materials' utility inside formal instructive settings and supports the learning targets framed by instructive establishments.

3. **Consolidating Intuitiveness and Commitment:**

   Intuitive components upgrade commitment and maintenance. Consolidating exercises, reenactments, and interactive media parts encourages dynamic support and builds up ideas. Intuitive instructive materials catch consideration as well as establish a unique learning climate.

4. **Advancing Decisive Reasoning and Critical thinking:**

   Compelling instructive materials go past repetition retention. They energize decisive reasoning and critical thinking abilities by introducing genuine situations, offering interesting conversation starters, and encouraging request based learning. This approach outfits students with abilities relevant past the homeroom.

5. **Social Responsiveness and Inclusivity:**

Social responsiveness is foremost in instructive material turn of events, guaranteeing that content is comprehensive and aware of different foundations. Perceiving and consolidating different social viewpoints enhances the growth opportunity, encouraging a feeling of having a place among understudies.

III. Creating Instructive Materials for Computerized Stages:

1. **E-Learning Modules and Online Assets:**

   The computerized period has introduced another rush of instructive conceivable outcomes. E-learning modules and online assets give adaptability in getting to instructive materials. These stages can offer sight and sound substance, intuitive appraisals, and cooperative devices that take care of different learning inclinations.

2. **Adjusting to Mixed Learning Conditions:**

Instructive materials for computerized stages are essential to the progress of mixed learning models, consolidating customary study hall guidance with on-line parts. This half and half methodology considers customized opportunities for growth, taking care of the necessities of individual students while keeping up with the advantages of face to face connections.

3. **Openness and Widespread Plan:**

Advanced instructive materials should focus on availability. General plan standards guarantee that materials are usable by people with different capacities and handicaps. This obligation to inclusivity broadens the range of instructive assets to a more extensive crowd.

IV. Local area Driven Instructive Material Turn of events:

1. **Drawing in Neighborhood People group:**

Compelling instructive materials resound with the nearby setting. Drawing in neighborhood networks in the advancement cycle guarantees that materials mirror the particular necessities, challenges, and social subtleties of the students. Local area inclusion encourages a feeling of pride and importance.

2. **Advancing Multilingual Instruction:**

In different networks, instructive materials that embrace multilingualism are fundamental. Creating assets in numerous dialects guarantees that language hindrances don't thwart admittance to training, encouraging a climate where etymological variety is commended.

3. **Tending to Financial Incongruities:**

Instructive materials can be intended to address financial incongruities. Drives giving free or minimal expense instructive assets, including reading material, exercise manuals, and computerized apparatuses, add to making everything fair and lessening instructive disparities.

V. Joint effort Between Instructive Establishments and Partners:

1. **Organizations with Instructive Establishments:**

Joint effort between instructive material engineers and foundations is vital for progress. Adjusting content to educational plan prerequisites, getting input from instructors, and understanding study hall elements guarantee that the materials flawlessly coordinate into formal schooling settings.

2. **Including Partners in the Advancement Cycle:**

Partner association, including instructors, guardians, and schooling policymakers, is fundamental. These people give significant bits of knowledge into the necessities of students, offer different viewpoints, and add to the general viability and importance of instructive materials.

VI. Specific Instructive Materials for Assorted Advancing Necessities:

1. **Comprehensive Training for Extraordinary Requirements:**

    Instructive materials should take care of the different necessities of students, incorporating those with unique requirements. Making assets that are versatile, giving elective organizations, and consolidating assistive innovations guarantees that schooling is comprehensive and available to all.

2. **Gifted and Capable Instruction:**

Fitting instructive materials for gifted and capable understudies is similarly significant. Offering progressed content, testing exercises, and valuable open doors for autonomous investigation upholds the novel learning necessities of successful people.

VII. Ceaseless Improvement and Variation:

1. **Input Circles and Iterative Plan:**

    Persistent improvement is a sign of successful instructive material turn of events. Laying out input circles with teachers, students, and different partners works with an iterative plan process. Standard assessments and updates guarantee that materials stay pertinent and lined up with developing instructive requirements.

2. **Adjusting to Mechanical Advances:**

Instructive materials should keep up to date with mechanical advances. Embracing arising advances, like computerized reasoning, augmented simulation, and versatile learning stages, takes into consideration the making of state of the art materials that influence the most recent instruments for improved growth opportunities.

VIII. Effect and Assessment of Instructive Materials:

1. **Estimating Learning Results:**

    The effect of instructive materials is surveyed through the estimation of learning results. Assessment measurements might incorporate state administered test scores, understudy execution, and subjective input from teachers and students. Vigorous assessment processes advise future cycles regarding instructive materials.

2. **Long haul Cultural Effect:**

The cultural effect of instructive materials reaches out past individual learning results. A knowledgeable people adds to cultural turn of events, monetary development, and the development of educated, connected with residents. Instructive materials assume an essential part in molding the direction of networks and social orders.

IX. Difficulties and Future Contemplations:

1. **Asset Limitations and Subsidizing:**

   Satisfactory subsidizing is vital for the turn of events and conveyance of excellent instructive materials. Asset requirements represent a test, especially in districts with restricted monetary assets. Procedures to get subsidizing and streamline asset use are fundamental.

2. **Advanced Separation and Innovative Imbalance:**

   The computerized partition stays a huge obstacle in guaranteeing fair admittance to instructive materials. Variations in innovation foundation and web access ruin the adequacy of computerized learning assets. Tending to innovative imbalance is basic for establishing comprehensive instructive conditions.

3. **Social Responsiveness and Worldwide Pertinence:**

Offsetting social responsiveness with worldwide pertinence is a continuous test. Instructive materials should be versatile to assorted social settings while giving substance that plans students to the globalized world. Finding some kind of harmony requires nonstop refinement and aversion to social subtleties.

7.2 Promoting swallow-friendly practices in urban planning

As urbanization keeps on reshaping scenes, it is fundamental to think about the effect on neighborhood natural life, including transitory birds like swallows. Swallows, known for their agile aeronautical trapeze artistry and bug control commitments, face difficulties in metropolitan conditions. Advancing swallow-accommodating practices in metropolitan arranging is vital to guaranteeing the prosperity of these avian species and keeping a reasonable metropolitan biological system.

1. **Safeguarding Settling Destinations:**

   One of the essential contemplations in swallow-accommodating metropolitan arranging is the safeguarding of appropriate settling locales. Swallows frequently construct their homes in protected areas, like roof, edges, or under spans. Consolidating plan components that emulate regular settling conditions, for example, giving edges or nooks in structures, upholds the continuation of swallow populaces in metropolitan regions.

2. **Diminishing Light Contamination:**

   Light contamination represents a danger to nighttime bugs, an essential food hotspot for swallows. Metropolitan arranging can coordinate methodologies to lessen light contamination, like introducing protected streetlamps and advancing energy-effective outside lighting. This not just advantages swallows by protecting their food source yet in addition adds to in general ecological preservation endeavors.

3. **Limiting Pesticide Use:**

Swallows contribute essentially to bother control by consuming tremendous amounts of bugs everyday. Metropolitan arranging drives can advance incorporated bother the executives works on, limiting the utilization of pesticides that might hurt swallow populaces by implication. Empowering regular bug control techniques upholds both the biological equilibrium and the prosperity of these insectivorous birds.

4. **Making Green Spaces:**

Incorporating green spaces inside metropolitan scenes gives various advantages to swallows. These regions not just deal potential settling destinations, like trees and bushes, yet additionally draw in bugs, improving the scavenging valuable open doors for swallows. Metropolitan arranging that focuses on green spaces adds to the in general natural soundness of the metropolitan climate and makes territories reasonable for swallows.

5. **Teaching People in general:**

Public mindfulness is a basic part of swallow-accommodating metropolitan preparation. Instructive projects and signage can educate occupants about the significance regarding swallows, their part in bother control, and the moves people can make to help these birds. Making a feeling of local area obligation cultivates a good climate for conjunction among people and swallows.

6. **Executing Building Plan Rules:**

Metropolitan arranging can consolidate building plan rules that think about the necessities of swallows. For instance, empowering the utilization of bird-accommodating glass and keeping away from structures that ruin swallow flight examples can limit impacts and aggravations. These rules add to the making of metropolitan spaces that are both practical for people and chivalrous of untamed life.

7. **Saving Water Bodies:**

Swallows are in many cases found close to water bodies where they can track down mud for building their homes and a dependable wellspring of bugs. Metropolitan arranging drives that monitor and safeguard water bodies add to the conservation of swallow living spaces. This incorporates overseeing water quality, forestalling contamination, and saving normal water highlights inside metropolitan settings.

7.3 Encouraging responsible tourism to protect swallow habitats

As worldwide travel keeps on developing, the effect of the travel industry on the climate, including natural life environments, turns out to be progressively huge. Swallows, with their fragile environments and transitory examples, are especially helpless against aggravations brought about by unreliable the travel industry. Empowering capable the travel industry isn't simply a question of saving regular magnificence yet additionally protecting the living spaces fundamental for the prosperity of swallow populaces. In this investigation, we dig into the significance of dependable the travel industry in safeguarding swallow environments and layout techniques to cultivate a manageable harmony among the travel industry and protection.

1. **Figuring out Swallow Natural surroundings:**

1. **Normal Settling Destinations:**

    Swallows frequently pick regular settling destinations, like precipices, trees, and under overhang or extensions. These natural surroundings give sanctuary, wellbeing, and closeness to reasonable scrounging regions. Understanding the particular necessities of swallows helps in recognizing regions where the travel industry might affect their settling and reproducing exercises.

2. **Rummaging Grounds:**

Swallows are insectivores, depending on bountiful bug populaces for food. Their scavenging grounds are normally close to water bodies, fields, or different places where bugs are copious. Dependable the travel industry ought to think about the effect of human exercises on these basic scavenging regions.

II. Challenges Presented by Flippant The travel industry:

1. **Aggravation to Settling Destinations:**

    Flippant the travel industry, set apart by exercises like clearly commotions, actual unsettling influences, and interruption into settling regions, can make critical pressure swallow populaces. Aggravations during the settling season might prompt home surrender, influencing regenerative achievement.

2. **Corruption of Scrounging Regions:**

    Unregulated the travel industry can prompt territory debasement, contamination, and changes in land utilize that adversely influence swallow scavenging grounds. Loss of bug rich environments can undermine the accessibility of nourishment for swallows, influencing their wellbeing and endurance.

3. **Impact Dangers:**

High-traffic traveler regions can present crash gambles for swallows, particularly those in flight. Structures, structures, and different deterrents in vacationer zones might prompt bird strikes, causing wounds or fatalities. Limiting these dangers is pivotal for the prosperity of swallow populaces.

III. Advantages of Dependable The travel industry for Swallow Natural surroundings:

1. **Saving Settling Locales:**

   Dependable the travel industry rehearses focus on the conservation of regular settling destinations. This incorporates executing rules to restrict human aggravations during the settling season, staying away from development in basic regions, and assigning safeguarded zones to guarantee the undisturbed rearing of swallows.

2. **Rationing Scrounging Grounds:**

   Reasonable the travel industry drives plan to monitor and safeguard swallow scrounging grounds. This includes limiting contamination, protecting water bodies, and laying out guidelines to forestall overdevelopment that could lessen the accessibility of bugs in these basic environments.

3. **Instructive Open doors:**

Capable the travel industry gives instructive open doors to guests to find out about the significance of swallow territories and the job these birds play in keeping up with biological equilibrium. Mindfulness projects can urge vacationers to capably see the value in the sensitive idea of these biological systems and act.

IV. Techniques for Empowering Capable The travel industry:

1. **Executing Overarching sets of principles:**

   Create and implement overarching sets of principles for sightseers in regions known to have swallow populaces. These rules can incorporate avoiding settling destinations, staying away from clearly commotions, and forgoing exercises that might upset the birds.

2. **Instructive Signage and Interpretive Projects:**

   Introduce instructive signage and foster interpretive projects in traveler regions to educate guests about the presence regarding swallows and the significance of dependable way of behaving. Mindfulness missions can cultivate a feeling of obligation and appreciation for the common habitat.

3. **Local area Commitment and Cooperation:**

   Draw in nearby networks in advancing capable the travel industry. Lay out organizations between preservation associations, nearby organizations, and the travel industry administrators to make a unified front for the insurance of swallow environments. Including people group guarantees that capable practices are socially delicate and manageable.

4. **The travel industry Arranging with Environmental Contemplations:**

Integrate environmental contemplations into the travel industry arranging. Direct intensive ecological effect appraisals prior to creating or extending traveler framework. This incorporates assessing expected influences on swallow environments and executing alleviation measures to limit aggravations.

5. **Laying out Cradle Zones:**

Assign cradle zones around swallow settling and scavenging destinations to restrict human access and likely unsettling influences. These safeguarded regions act as safe-havens where swallows can take part in fundamental exercises without superfluous disturbances from the travel industry related exercises.

6. **Advancing Low-Effect The travel industry:**

Support low-influence the travel industry rehearses that focus on the preservation of regular natural surroundings. This might incorporate advancing bird-watching exercises, directed visits with prepared naturalists, and eco-accommodating facilities that limit their ecological impression.

V. Worldwide Participation for Swallow Protection:

1. **Global Joint effort:**

Swallows are transient birds that cross tremendous distances, making global cooperation vital for their preservation. Nations along transient courses should arrange endeavors to carry out capable the travel industry rehearses that safeguard swallow natural surroundings and guarantee their protected section.

2. **Sharing Prescribed procedures:**

Make stages for the sharing of best practices in swallow protection through global discussions, gatherings, and cooperative exploration drives. Trading information and encounters permits countries to gain from one another and execute compelling systems for the assurance of swallow living spaces.

VI. Exploration and Checking:

1. **Consistent Checking of Swallow Populaces:**

Carry out consistent observing projects to evaluate the wellbeing and status of swallow populaces in regions visited by sightseers. Examination can assist with distinguishing explicit dangers, measure the progress of preservation endeavors, and adjust systems to changing biological circumstances.

2. **Concentrating on the Effect of The travel industry:**

Lead examination to figure out the effect of the travel industry on swallow environments. This includes contemplating settling achievement rates, rummaging examples, and populace elements in regions presented to various degrees of the travel industry. Research discoveries can illuminate designated preservation systems.

VII. Benefits Past Swallow Protection:

1. **Monetary Advantages for Neighborhood People group:**
   Capable the travel industry rehearses add to swallow protection as well as yield monetary advantages for nearby networks. Manageable the travel industry can draw in eco-cognizant voyagers, set out work open doors, and backing neighborhood organizations that focus on natural obligation.

2. **Conservation of Biodiversity:**
   Endeavors to safeguard swallow natural surroundings add to the protection of generally speaking biodiversity. Sound biological systems that help swallow populaces likewise benefit other untamed life species, making a stronger and adjusted common habitat.

3. **Improving Vacationer Encounters:**

Mindful the travel industry upgrades the nature of vacationer encounters. Guests who take part in reasonable practices and witness the excellence of normal territories, remembering swallows for their regular habitat, frequently gain a more profound appreciation for the objections they investigate.

Chapter 8

Monitoring And Research

Observing and research assume crucial parts in our journey to comprehend and support the fragile harmony between normal environments and human exercises. These undertakings give bits of knowledge into the many-sided elements of our current circumstance, empowering informed decision-production for preservation, asset the executives, and supportable turn of events. In this investigation, we dig into the meaning of checking and research, the assorted approaches utilized, and the groundbreaking effect of these undertakings on the worldwide scene.

1. **Figuring out the Meaning of Checking and Exploration:**
1. **Biological system Wellbeing and Biodiversity:**

    Observing and research are instrumental in evaluating the wellbeing of environments and the variety of life inside them. By concentrating on greenery, analysts gain significant experiences into the general prosperity of conditions, distinguishing possible dangers and illuminating preservation methodologies.

2. **Environmental Change and Ecological Movements:**

    Checking and research are vital apparatuses for following environmental change and its consequences for the climate. Information gathered through long haul studies add to how we might interpret moving atmospheric conditions, climbing temperatures, and their effects on environments, working with the advancement of versatile methodologies.

3. **Human-Climate Cooperations:**

    Understanding the cooperations between human exercises and the climate is fundamental for supportable turn of events. Checking and research shed light on the results of human activities, assisting policymakers and networks with pursuing informed choices to limit adverse consequences and advance mindful practices.

4. **Asset The executives and Preservation:**

Compelling asset the board depends on exact data about the condition of regular assets. Through checking and research, researchers can survey the accessibility and supportability of assets, directing protection endeavors and guaranteeing the capable utilization of normal resources.

II. Techniques in Checking and Exploration:

1. **Remote Detecting and Satellite Innovation:**

   Remote detecting and satellite innovation give an elevated perspective of the Earth, permitting researchers to screen huge scope natural changes. From deforestation and land-use changes to following environment designs, these apparatuses offer important information for exhaustive checking and research.

2. **Ground-Based Observing:**

   Ground-put together checking includes with respect to site information assortment through hands on work, sensor establishments, and direct perceptions. This active methodology gives definite data about nearby biological systems, including biodiversity evaluations, water quality estimations, and soil investigations.

3. **Resident Science and Publicly supporting:**

   Resident science draws in general society in logical exploration, utilizing the force of huge scope information assortment. Through portable applications and online stages, people can contribute perceptions on natural life, environment conditions, and ecological changes, growing the span and profundity of observing endeavors.

4. **Research facility Investigations and Controlled Examinations:**

   Lab tries and controlled investigations permit scientists to segregate explicit factors and study their belongings under controlled conditions. These strategies are especially valuable for figuring out circumstances and logical results connections, testing speculations, and investigating central logical standards.

5. **Demonstrating and Reenactment:**

Demonstrating and reenactment include the production of numerical models to recreate complex ecological cycles. These models assist scientists with foreseeing future situations, survey possible effects, and test the viability of various administration methodologies without straightforwardly controlling genuine frameworks.

III. Uses of Observing and Exploration:

1. **Environment Observing and Preservation:**

   Checking biological systems gives fundamental information to preservation endeavors. Whether following the populace elements of imperiled species, evaluating the soundness of coral reefs, or concentrating on the effect of obtrusive species, progressing observing aides preservation practices to shield biodiversity.

2. **Environment Checking and Variation:**

Constant checking of environment pointers, like temperature, precipitation, and ocean levels, advises our comprehension regarding environmental change. This information is essential for creating variation techniques, alleviating the effects of environment related occasions, and figuring out arrangements to decrease ozone depleting substance emanations.

3. **Regular Asset The board:**

Observing is indispensable for the reasonable administration of regular assets. Whether evaluating fisheries, checking water quality in streams, or following deforestation rates, research-driven experiences guide arrangements and practices that offset human requirements with ecological safeguarding.

4. **Human Wellbeing and Natural Openness:**

Examination into the associations between the climate and human wellbeing is an arising field. Checking air and water quality, concentrating on the effect of poisons, and understanding the spread of vector-borne infections give basic data to shielding human prosperity.

5. **Metropolitan Preparation and Savvy Urban communities:**

Observing and research add to the improvement of shrewd urban areas and reasonable metropolitan preparation. By following energy utilization, air contamination, and traffic examples, specialists and metropolitan organizers can upgrade asset use, improve public administrations, and establish better living conditions.

IV. The Job of Enormous Information and Innovation:

1. **Enormous Information Investigation:**

The coming of enormous information examination has upset observing and research abilities. Huge datasets, produced through remote detecting, resident science, and different sources, empower scientists to extricate designs, recognize patterns, and settle on information driven choices for natural administration.

2. **Man-made brainpower and AI:**

Man-made brainpower (artificial intelligence) and AI (ML) calculations break down tremendous datasets, computerizing design acknowledgment and information translation. In natural exploration, computer based intelligence and ML add to species ID, environment displaying, and anticipating biological changes in light of authentic information.

3. **Web of Things (IoT) and Sensor Organizations:**

IoT gadgets and sensor networks upgrade continuous observing abilities. Conveying sensors in different conditions considers persistent information assortment on boundaries like temperature, moistness, and toxin levels, giving a dynamic and nitty gritty image of natural circumstances.

4. **Blockchain for Natural Information Respectability:**

Blockchain innovation guarantees the uprightness and straightforwardness of ecological information. By making a protected and decentralized record, blockchain mitigates concerns connected with information altering and cultivates trust in the exactness of data gathered through observing and research.

V. Challenges in Observing and Exploration:

1. **Information Quality and Normalization:**

Keeping up with information quality and normalization across assorted checking techniques can challenge. Irregularities in information assortment and announcing can thwart the similarity of results, affecting the unwavering quality of ends drawn from various examinations.

2. **Monetary Imperatives:**

Satisfactory financing is fundamental for supported checking and research endeavors. Monetary requirements might restrict the extent of studies, preventing the capacity to assemble complete information and lead long haul observing undertakings.

3. **Mechanical Progressions and Moral Contemplations:**

The quick speed of mechanical headways raises moral contemplations. Adjusting the advantages of new innovations with potential protection issues, information security concerns, and the moral utilization of computer based intelligence and AI is a continuous test.

4. **Worldwide Cooperation and Information Sharing:**

Accomplishing exhaustive bits of knowledge into worldwide natural issues requires global coordinated effort and information sharing. Conquering hindrances connected with information access, sharing conventions, and contrasting examination plans is vital for an all encompassing comprehension of mind boggling ecological difficulties.

VI. Future Patterns and Contemplations:

1. **Incorporation of Satellite Advancements:**

Proceeded with progressions in satellite advancements, including higher-goal symbolism and upgraded information handling capacities, will additionally work on our capacity to screen huge scope natural changes and track biodiversity designs.

2. **Growing Resident Science Drives:**

   The job of resident science is supposed to grow, with additional people adding to information assortment endeavors. Further developed availability to logical apparatuses, portable applications, and instructive projects will engage residents to take part in natural observing effectively.

3. **Headways in Natural Genomics:**

   Natural genomics, concentrating on the hereditary material in ecological examples, holds extraordinary potential for observing biodiversity and grasping environments. DNA examination of soil, water, and air tests can give an abundance of data about the species present in a given climate.

4. **Improved Prescient Demonstrating:**

   Prescient demonstrating will turn out to be more modern with the reconciliation of cutting edge computational strategies. AI calculations will refine prescient models, offering more exact projections of natural changes and taking into account proactive direction.

5. **Accentuation on Interdisciplinary Exploration:**

Interdisciplinary methodologies that unite scientists from different fields will turn out to be progressively significant. Joint efforts between biologists, information researchers, sociologists, and policymakers will improve the comprehensive comprehension of perplexing ecological issues.

VII. The Crossing point of Observing and Exploration with Strategy and Promotion:

1. **Impacting Strategy Choices:**

   Information created through observing and research act as significant contributions for policymaking. Logical proof illuminates strategy choices connected with environmental change, preservation, asset the board, and other natural worries, directing states in taking on compelling techniques.

2. **Support for Ecological Stewardship:**

   The discoveries of exploration and observing endeavors frequently fuel natural promotion. Researchers and specialists assume a vital part in bringing issues to light about basic issues, preparing public help, and supporting for strategies that focus on maintainability and the security of environments.

3. **Estimating the Effect of Approaches:**

Checking and research take into account the appraisal of strategy viability. By following natural pointers over the long haul, analysts can assess the effect of carried out arrangements, distinguish regions for development, and contribute significant experiences to the iterative policymaking process.

8.1Establishing long-term monitoring programs for swallow populations

Swallows, with their elegant flight and fundamental job in controlling bug populaces, are basic parts of environments around the world. In any case, these transitory birds face different dangers, going from living space misfortune to environmental change. Laying out long haul checking programs for swallow populaces is pivotal for figuring out their elements, recognizing expected dangers, and executing designated protection measures. In this investigation, we dig into the significance of such observing drives, the philosophies in question, and the advantages they bring to the protection of these avian species.

1. **Meaning of Long haul Observing for Swallow Populaces:**

1. **Populace Patterns and Elements:**

   Long haul observing gives experiences into the patterns and elements of swallow populaces overstretched periods. By following populace sizes, reproducing achievement, and dissemination designs, scientists can distinguish variances and possible causes, adding to a more profound comprehension of the general soundness of swallow populaces.

2. **Movement Examples and Courses:**

   Swallows attempt broad movements, navigating mainlands looking for appropriate reproducing and searching grounds. Long haul checking empowers the following of movement examples and courses, revealing insight into the difficulties looked during relocation and possible dangers along these basic excursions.

3. **Rearing Achievement and Settling Ways of behaving:**

   Observing rearing achievement and settling ways of behaving is fundamental for evaluating the regenerative wellbeing of swallow populaces. Long haul studies permit scientists to investigate factors affecting home achievement, like predation, atmospheric conditions, and the accessibility of appropriate settling destinations.

4. **Effect of Natural Changes:**

Swallows are delicate to ecological changes, remembering adjustments for environment and territory. Long haul checking programs give the information expected to comprehend what these progressions mean for swallow populaces, illuminating protection techniques to relieve the impacts of elements, for example, environmental change, living space misfortune, and contamination.

II. Systems in Long haul Swallow Checking:

1. **Home Box Projects:**

   Introducing home boxes in essential areas considers the perception of swallow settling ways of behaving and gives a controlled climate to checking reproducing achievement. Specialists can gather information on grasp sizes, youngster rates, and the general soundness of settling populaces.

2. **Bird Banding and Imprint Recover Studies:**

Bird banding includes appending interesting identifiers to individual birds, working with the following of their developments and endurance rates over the long run. Mark-recover studies, where joined birds are caught, stamped, and afterward delivered, give vital information on populace size, death rates, and movement designs.

3. **Reviews and Resident Science Drives:**

Ordinary reviews led by researchers, preservation associations, and resident researchers add to long haul checking endeavors. Resident science drives connect with people in general in information assortment, widening the geographic extent of checking and giving significant data on swallow populaces across different districts.

4. **Remote Detecting Innovations:**

Remote detecting innovations, including satellite symbolism and automated elevated vehicles (UAVs), offer effective methods for observing enormous scope swallow environments. These advancements can give experiences into environment changes, land-use examples, and likely dangers to swallow populaces.

5. **Acoustic Observing:**

Acoustic observing includes recording and investigating bird vocalizations, which can give data on swallow presence, movement levels, and likely correspondence between people. This harmless technique is especially helpful for checking swallow populaces in testing or far off environments.

III. Advantages of Long haul Observing Projects for Swallow Protection:

1. **Early Discovery of Dangers:**

Long haul checking empowers the early recognition of dangers to swallow populaces. Whether it be living space debasement, changes in bug overflow, or arising illnesses, constant checking permits moderates to distinguish and address dangers before they heighten.

2. **Versatile Protection Systems:**

Long haul information gives an establishment to versatile protection systems. By understanding how swallow populaces answer natural changes, protectionists can foster designated mediations, like territory reclamation, hunter the board, or environment transformation measures, to help the strength of these bird species.

3. **Logical Bits of knowledge into Conduct and Biology:**

Expanded checking programs offer logical bits of knowledge into the way of behaving and environment of swallows. Scientists can disentangle complex inquiries connected with mate choice, relocation courses, and the transaction between natural variables and regenerative achievement, adding to a complete comprehension of these avian species.

4. **Preservation Training and Effort:**

Long haul checking programs present open doors for preservation training and effort. Imparting discoveries to people in general, schools, and neighborhood networks cultivates mindfulness about the significance of swallows and the difficulties they face. Taught people group are bound to participate in preservation endeavors and backing drives to safeguard swallow living spaces.

IV. Difficulties and Contemplations in Long haul Observing:

1. **Asset Escalation:**

Long haul observing requires critical assets, including financing, staff, and innovative foundation. Getting progressing support for observing projects is a test that requires joint effort between scientists, protection associations, and legislative organizations.

2. **Information Normalization and Quality:**

Keeping up with predictable information principles over a lengthy period is fundamental for the dependability of long haul observing endeavors. Challenges connected with changes in systems, spectator predisposition, and information quality should be addressed to guarantee the exactness and similarity of information gathered over the long haul.

3. **Populace Elements and Movement Difficulties:**

Swallows display complex populace elements and attempt broad movements, introducing difficulties in following people across enormous geographic regions. Mechanical progressions, for example, geolocators and satellite following, can support conquering these difficulties yet may represent their own constraints.

4. **Human Unsettling influences and Settling Achievement:**

Swallows are helpless to human aggravations, and observing settling achievement can be trying because of potential interruptions brought about by human exercises. Carrying out measures to limit aggravations, for example, cradle zones around settling locales, is significant for exact information assortment.

V. Future Bearings and Improvements in Swallow Observing:

1. **Combination of Cutting edge innovations:**

Continuous progressions in advancements, including scaled down GPS beacons and computerized reasoning for information examination, offer chances to upgrade the productivity and extent of swallow checking programs. These advances can give continuous information and more exact bits of knowledge into swallow conduct.

2. **Cooperative Global Endeavors:**

Swallows are transient birds that cross huge distances and may traverse various nations during their yearly relocations. Cooperative worldwide endeavors are fundamental for following their total life cycles, understanding dangers along relocation courses, and organizing protection techniques on a worldwide scale.

3. **Tackling Resident Science and Local area Inclusion:**

The job of resident science can be extended, with local area contribution assuming a vital part in observing swallow populaces. Drawing in neighborhood networks in information assortment, giving instructive projects, and cultivating a feeling of stewardship can fortify long haul checking drives.

4. **Long haul Exploration Practice Associations:**

Laying out long haul associations between analysts, preservation professionals, and policymakers is vital. These associations can guarantee that logical discoveries are converted into noteworthy preservation measures, adding to the supported prosperity of swallow populaces.

8.2 Funding and supporting research on swallow behavior and ecology

Swallows, with their aeronautical trapeze artistry and huge natural jobs, dazzle the two researchers and lovers the same. Understanding the way of behaving and environment of these transitory birds is critical for their preservation and adds to more extensive bits of knowledge into biological system elements. Financing and supporting examination on swallow conduct and nature are imperative parts of this undertaking, giving the assets important to unwind the complexities of their lives. In this investigation, we dive into the significance of such examination, the difficulties confronted, and the roads for encouraging supported help.

1. **Significance of Exploration on Swallow Conduct and Biology:**

1. **Biological Jobs:**

Swallows assume key parts in keeping up with biological equilibrium by adding to bug control. Their unquenchable hunger for bugs makes them significant partners in directing bug populaces, helping horticulture and biological systems.

2. **Relocation Examples:**

Swallows are eminent for their noteworthy movements, covering huge distances among reproducing and wintering grounds. Research on their movement designs reveals the difficulties they face during these excursions and illuminates preservation endeavors to safeguard basic visit locales.

3. **Conceptive Science:**

Understanding the conceptive science of swallows is fundamental for protection techniques. Research on settling ways of behaving, rearing achievement, and variables affecting conceptive wellbeing gives bits of knowledge into the flexibility of populaces and expected dangers to their manageability.

4. **Effect of Natural Changes:**

Swallows are delicate to natural changes, making them important marks of biological system wellbeing. Research on how they answer modifications in environment, natural surroundings, and human exercises adds to how we might interpret more extensive biological movements.

II. **Challenges in Financing Exploration on Swallow Conduct and Biology:**

1. **Restricted Financing Sources:**

Financing for research on swallows might be restricted, as these birds may not get as much consideration as bigger or more charming species. Getting predictable and sufficient financing is a test that scientists face in leading long haul review.

2. **Intricacy of Exploration:**

Concentrating on swallow conduct and environment can be intricate because of their transitory nature, high versatility, and aversion to unsettling influence. Research activities might require cutting edge innovations, for example, GPS beacons, which can add to inflated costs.

3. **Interdisciplinary Nature:**

Exhaustive examination on swallows frequently requires an interdisciplinary methodology, including ornithologists, biologists, climatologists, and that's just the beginning. Joint efforts across assorted fields might confront difficulties in adjusting research objectives and approaches.

4. **Restricted Exploration Framework:**

In districts where swallow populaces are bountiful, there might be restricted examination framework. Absence of admittance to explore offices, field stations, and logical hardware can block the advancement of concentrates on swallow conduct and biology.

III. **Roads for Subsidizing and Supporting Exploration:**

1. **Government Awards and Subsidizing Organizations:**

Government awards and subsidizing organizations devoted to untamed life preservation and environmental exploration can act as urgent wellsprings of monetary help. Analysts can apply for awards to support explicit undertakings or long haul checking programs zeroed in on swallow conduct and environment.

2. **Not-for-profit Associations and Establishments:**

Philanthropic associations and establishments with an emphasis on bird protection and biodiversity might offer awards and backing for research on swallows. These substances frequently focus on projects that add to the comprehension and protection of avian species.

3. **Corporate Sponsorships and Organizations:**

Laying out organizations with enterprises, particularly those with interests lined up with natural preservation, can give subsidizing to explore drives. Corporate sponsorships might uphold concentrates on swallow conduct and environment as a feature of their corporate social obligation endeavors.

4. **Crowdfunding and Public Help:**

Scientists can investigate crowdfunding stages to raise assets for explicit activities on swallow conduct and environment. Connecting with the general population through outreach endeavors, instructive projects, and resident science drives can create backing and subsidizing from people energetic about bird preservation.

5. **Scholastic Joint efforts and Exploration Consortia:**

Teaming up with scholastic establishments and taking part in research consortia can offer admittance to shared assets, offices, and aptitude. Joint endeavors between colleges, research focuses, and associations can upgrade the general effect of exploration on swallow conduct and nature.

IV. Advancing Public Mindfulness and Commitment:

1. **Instructive Projects and Effort:**

Expanding public mindfulness about the significance of swallow exploration can earn support from people and networks. Instructive projects, studios, and effort drives can feature the natural meaning of swallows and the requirement for supported research endeavors.

2. **Resident Science Drives:**

Including the general population in information assortment through resident science drives contributes significant data as well as cultivates a feeling of pride and backing for research tries. Giving open doors to residents to take part in observing projects reinforces the association among analysts and the more extensive local area.

3. **Media and Correspondence Methodologies:**

Actually conveying research discoveries through different media channels, including conventional and computerized stages, can earn public premium and backing. Drawing in narrating, visuals, and narratives can convey the significance of grasping swallow conduct and nature to a more extensive crowd.

4. **Organizations with Nature Stores and Preservation Regions:**

Teaming up with nature stores and preservation regions can furnish analysts with admittance to safeguarded environments and assets. Laying out associations with associations dealing with these areas can upgrade the achievability of long haul observing projects.

V. Defeating Difficulties and Upgrading Exploration Effect:

1. **Systems administration and Joint effort:**

Building solid organizations inside established researchers and encouraging coordinated efforts across disciplines can conquer the difficulties presented by the interdisciplinary idea of swallow research. Sharing mastery and assets upgrades the general effect of review.

2. **Enhancing Financing Sources:**

Analysts can moderate the gamble of restricted financing by differentiating their sources. Investigating potential open doors from different channels, for example, government awards, charitable associations, and public commitment drives, decreases reliance on a solitary financing stream.

3. **Open Access and Information Sharing:**

Advancing open-access distributions and imparting research information to mainstream researchers encourages joint effort and builds the perceivability of examination on swallow conduct and biology. This approach adds to the aggregate information base and empowers more extensive help.

4. **Utilizing Innovation and Creative Techniques:**

Embracing mechanical headways, like remote detecting, acoustic observing, and information investigation, can upgrade the proficiency of swallow research. Imaginative techniques can address the intricacies of concentrating on these birds, making research more financially savvy and significant.

8.3 Utilizing technology for real-time monitoring and data collection

In the domain of natural examination and protection, mechanical headways have introduced another period of effectiveness and accuracy. One especially effective application lies in the domain of continuous checking and information assortment, altering the manner in which specialists accumulate data about the normal world. This change is particularly obvious in the investigation of avian species like swallows, where understanding their way of behaving and nature requests consistent and exact information. Here, we investigate the advantages and developments related with using innovation for ongoing observing and information assortment with regards to swallow research.

Constant observing use state of the art innovations to give moment admittance to information, offering scientists a dynamic and extensive perspective on biological systems. In the investigation of swallow populaces, this approach empowers researchers to assemble data without disturbances, giving experiences into the birds' ways of behaving, relocation examples, and reactions to ecological changes.

One key innovation adding to continuous observing is the utilization of GPS trackers and geolocators. These gadgets, frequently sent on individual swallows, permit specialists to follow the birds' developments with exceptional accuracy. By gathering information on relocation courses, visit areas, and everyday developments, researchers gain an all encompassing comprehension of swallow conduct and biology. This innovation works with the checking of whole populaces as well as gives bits of knowledge into individual bird encounters, enhancing the profundity of examination.

Notwithstanding GPS innovation, remote detecting devices like satellite symbolism and automated flying vehicles (UAVs) assume a significant part continuously observing. These innovations offer an elevated perspective of enormous scope natural surroundings, giving specialists important information ashore use, territory changes, and possible dangers. With regards to swallow protection, this constant spatial data supports recognizing basic settling and scrounging locales, evaluating natural surroundings wellbeing, and executing convenient intercessions.

Acoustic observing addresses one more wilderness progressively information assortment for swallow research. Conveying progressed recording gadgets fit for catching bird vocalizations permits specialists to examine ongoing data about swallow presence, correspondence, and possibly, feelings of anxiety. This painless methodology upgrades the comprehension of what human exercises mean for swallow conduct and nature.

The combination of information examination and man-made consciousness (simulated intelligence) further intensifies the utility of ongoing observing. Artificial intelligence calculations can process immense datasets, recognizing examples, connections, and peculiarities that could slip through the cracks with customary strategies. This scientific power empowers specialists to draw significant experiences from the nonstop stream of information produced by ongoing observing frameworks.

The advantages of using innovation for continuous observing and information assortment reach out past the logical domain. Preservation endeavors can be more responsive and versatile, with the capacity to execute intercessions in light of expert data. This quickness is especially pivotal in tending to arising dangers, for example, territory misfortune or environment actuated changes, which can affect swallow populaces.

Chapter 9

Conclusion

In the excursion through the different scenes of difficulties and open doors, the investigation of subjects going from ecological preservation and mechanical developments to instructive effort and the complexities of swallow conduct has given a far reaching point of view on the complicated trap of our reality. As we come to the end result, it becomes obvious that the difficulties we face are entwined with the potential open doors that emerge when we take a stab at a supportable and amicable concurrence with our current circumstance.

Natural Protection: A Source of inspiration

The call for ecological preservation repeats uproariously despite remarkable difficulties, for example, environmental change, biodiversity misfortune, and living space corruption. The investigation of methodologies, from advancing capable the travel industry and swallow-accommodating metropolitan wanting to observing environments and exploring holes in our grasping, highlights the earnestness of aggregate activity. Obviously defending the fragile equilibrium of our planet requires a comprehensive methodology that joins logical meticulousness, mechanical development, and informed policymaking.

Mechanical Developments: Forming What's in store

The material of protection is advancing, hued by the strokes of mechanical developments. From using computerized reasoning for information examination to utilizing satellite advancements for ongoing observing, the mix of innovation into ecological exploration is reclassifying the conceivable outcomes. As we explore the strange waters representing things to come, the proceeded with improvement and utilization of these developments hold the commitment of more profound experiences, more successful protection methodologies, and a more economical connection among mankind and the regular world.

Instructive Effort: Sustaining Stewards of the Earth

Schooling arises as an incredible asset in the stockpile of preservation. Instructive projects and effort drives are fundamental for cultivating mindfulness, moving a feeling of obligation, and supporting an age of natural stewards. The excursion through instructive projects and the improvement of materials for schools and networks features the significance of enabling people with information, ingraining a feeling of marvel, and supporting an association with the climate. As we look forward, putting resources into training stays a foundation for manageable turn of events and the development of a worldwide local area that qualities and safeguards our planet.

Swallow Conduct and Environment: Unwinding Nature's Embroidery

The investigation of swallow conduct and biology offers a microcosmic view into the complexities of the regular world. By digging into the difficulties looked by swallow populaces, the procedures utilized in their review, and the significance of long haul observing, we uncover important illustrations that stretch out past the avian domain. The narrative of swallows turns into an illustration for the interconnectedness of every living being and the fragile dance among people and the climate. The examples gained from concentrating on swallows reverberate in the more extensive setting of biodiversity protection and the safeguarding of environmental equilibrium.

Fitting Difficulties and Valuable open doors

In the orchestra of difficulties and valuable open doors, the finishing up notes welcome us to a reflection on the interconnectedness of our activities and their repercussions in the world. An update difficulties are not unrealistic road obstructions yet rather entryways to development, variation, and strength. Open doors, when seized with goal and prescience, become impetuses for positive change and economical turn of events.

What's in store holds the two vulnerabilities and commitments. Environment designs are moving, biological systems are developing, and human social orders are exploring unfamiliar domains. Notwithstanding, inside this powerful scene lies the potential for change. The difficulties we face today propel us to reconsider our relationship with the climate, reevaluate our utilization designs, and rethink the manners by which we coincide with different species.

As we make progress toward an agreeable conjunction with nature, joint effort arises as the foundation of our process forward. Whether it is through interdisciplinary examination drives, worldwide preservation associations, or local area driven endeavors, the aggregate force of people, associations, and countries is vital to exploring the skyline of potential outcomes. The difficulties we defy are not restricted by lines or teaches; they request cooperative and comprehensive arrangements that rise above political, social, and disciplinary limits.

9.1 Summarizing key findings and recommendations

The investigation of future difficulties and potential open doors, mechanical developments, instructive effort, and the complexities of swallow conduct has enlightened the multi-layered nature of our relationship with the climate. From a perspective that incorporates preservation, advancement, training, and the fragile dance of nature's occupants, key discoveries arise, offering important experiences for reasonable turn of events.

Grasping Future Difficulties and Valuable open doors:

The examination of future difficulties highlights the basic requirement for proactive techniques to resolve ecological issues. Environmental change, biodiversity misfortune, and living space corruption present complex difficulties, yet they additionally divulge amazing open doors for creative arrangements. The key focal point is that these difficulties are not unrealistic boundaries but instead passages to extraordinary activity. Through essential preparation and worldwide coordinated effort, we can bridle the potential inside difficulties to drive positive change.

Mechanical Advancements: Changing Preservation Endeavors:

The reconciliation of innovation into natural exploration has re-imagined the scene of preservation. From the usage of man-made brainpower and satellite advancements to constant checking, mechanical developments give extraordinary instruments to understanding and saving biological systems. The key finding is that continuous progressions in innovation offer a guide for more successful preservation endeavors. As we explore the future, the proceeded with advancement and utilization of these developments stand as points of support for informed independent direction and practical asset the executives.

Instructive Effort: Engaging Ecological Stewards:

The excursion through instructive projects and effort drives underscores the vital job of training in encouraging natural mindfulness. Key discoveries feature that putting resources into training isn't just a way to scatter data however an impetus for sustaining an age of ecological stewards. The commitment of networks, the improvement of instructive materials, and the advancement of resident science drives add to building an underpinning of information and obligation to economical practices.

Swallow Conduct and Biology: Examples from Nature's Pilots:

The investigation of swallow conduct fills in as a microcosm for grasping more extensive natural elements. Key discoveries uncover the complicated connection among swallows and their current circumstance, stressing the requirement for long haul observing to follow populace patterns, relocation designs, and settling ways of behaving. The difficulties looked by swallows equal those experienced by various species, underlining the interconnectedness of biodiversity preservation and the fragile equilibrium expected for the concurrence of different living things.

Suggestions for Economical Turn of events:

1. **Incorporated Preservation Procedures:**

   To address future difficulties, basic to embrace incorporated preservation techniques think about the interconnected idea of natural issues. This includes cultivating coordinated efforts between states, non-legislative associations, and nearby networks to foster far reaching approaches that tackle environmental change, territory safeguarding, and biodiversity protection all the while.

2. **Proceeded with Interest in Mechanical Headways:**

   The discoveries highlight the significance of supported interest in mechanical advancements for natural observing. Legislatures, confidential ventures, and examination foundations ought to focus on the turn of events and arrangement of trend setting innovations, including man-made reasoning, remote detecting, and constant observing devices, to improve how we might interpret environments and guide powerful preservation endeavors.

3. **Reinforcing Natural Training:**

   The vital action item from instructive effort drives is the need to fortify natural training at all levels. State run administrations and instructive organizations ought to apportion assets to foster far reaching ecological educational plans, advance open air opportunities for growth, and coordinate supportability standards into standard training. Furthermore, cultivating associations with local area associations and utilizing advanced stages can broaden the scope of ecological training programs.

4. **Long haul Observing Projects:**

The illustrations gained from concentrating on swallow conduct underscore the significance of laying out and keeping up with long haul observing projects for key species. Protection associations, specialists, and legislative offices ought to team up to execute and finance drives that track populace patterns, relocation courses, and territory changes overstretched periods. These projects are fundamental for adjusting preservation systems to developing natural circumstances.

9.2 Encouraging readers to take action in swallow conservation

The charming trip of swallows, with their elegant moves and fundamental biological jobs, requires our consideration and dynamic association in their protection. As we disentangle the intricacies of their way of behaving, comprehend the difficulties they face, and investigate the interconnectedness of their lives with our current circumstance, the basic to make a move turns out to be clear. In this source of inspiration, we dive into the ways people, networks, and worldwide residents can add to the protection of swallows and their environments, encouraging an aggregate obligation to safeguarding these avian marvels.

1. **Bring issues to light:**

   Schooling is the foundation of activity. Begin by bringing issues to light about the significance of swallows and the dangers they experience. Share data through web-based entertainment, local area occasions, and instructive projects. Stress the job swallows play in bother control, keeping up with environmental equilibrium, and their emblematic importance in our normal world. By building mindfulness, you establish the groundwork for informed activity.

2. **Make Swallow-Accommodating Spaces:**

   Change your quick environmental elements into inviting territories for swallows. Introduce home boxes in reasonable areas, giving places of refuge to settling and raising their young. Guarantee these spaces are liberated from unsettling influences, permitting swallows to flourish without pointless pressure. Support others locally to go with the same pattern, encouraging an organization of swallow-accommodating conditions.

3. **Take part in Resident Science Drives:**

   Add to logical information by taking part in resident science drives zeroed in on swallow checking. Join programs that include information assortment on swallow populaces, settling ways of behaving, and movement designs. By turning into a resident researcher, you effectively add to progressing research endeavors, giving significant data to researchers and preservationists.

4. **Support Protection Associations:**

   Numerous associations are committed to the preservation of birds and their environments. Support these drives through gifts, charitable effort, or dynamic cooperation in their projects. These associations assume a significant part in promotion, living space rebuilding, and exploration. Your help adds to their capacity to execute viable protection procedures.

5. **Embrace Manageable Practices:**

   Embrace maintainable practices in your everyday existence to relieve more extensive natural dangers. Lessen your carbon impression, reuse mindfully, and support maintainable agrarian practices. Swallows, in the same way as other different species, are affected by natural changes, and embracing eco-accommodating propensities adds to the more extensive endeavors in safeguarding their territories.

6. **Participate in Swallow-Accommodating Metropolitan Preparation:**

   Advocate for swallow-accommodating metropolitan preparation locally. Work with neighborhood specialists and designers to think about the requirements of swallows while arranging development projects. Integrate green spaces, keep up with vast water sources, and make support zones around settling destinations. By effectively partaking in the arranging system, you add to the formation of metropolitan conditions that help both human and avian populaces.

7. **Instruct the Future:**

Motivate people in the future to become stewards of the climate. Draw in with schools, instructive foundations, and youth associations to coordinate ecological training into educational plans. Energize open air growth opportunities and bird-watching exercises. Ingrain a feeling of obligation and association with nature, cultivating an age that qualities and safeguards the biodiversity of our planet.

8. **Advocate for Strategy Changes:**

Be a voice for swallows for a bigger scope by pushing for strategy changes that advance living space insurance, preservation, and economical practices. Draw in with policymakers, go to formal reviews, and join promotion bunches committed to ecological issues. By effectively taking part in the political cycle, you add to the formation of strategies that focus on the prosperity of swallow populaces.

9. **Team up with Neighborhood People group:**

Produce organizations with neighborhood networks to make an organization of people committed to swallow protection. Arrange people group occasions, studios, and tidy up drives that feature the significance of protecting swallow environments. Team up with different gatherings, including mortgage holders' affiliations, schools, and organizations, to make an aggregate effect.

10. **Record and Offer Examples of overcoming adversity:**

Celebrate triumphs in swallow preservation and offer these accounts with a more extensive crowd. Feature occasions where networks, associations, or people emphatically affect swallow populaces. These examples of overcoming adversity act as motivation and inspiration for others to make a move, encouraging a feeling of aggregate accomplishment.

9.3 Emphasizing the collective responsibility in preserving these vital bird species

The sensitive dance of swallows in our skies isn't just a scene of nature however a vital component in keeping up with the environmental equilibrium of our planet. As we investigate the difficulties these crucial bird species face and the amazing open doors for protection, the resonating topic arises — the aggregate liability we as a whole offer in guaranteeing the proceeded with presence and prosperity of these momentous avian miracles.

Grasping Swallows as Fundamental Patrons:

Swallows are not simply fleeting guests in our environments; they assume an essential part in the fragile embroidery of nature. With their ravenous craving for bugs, they contribute altogether to bug control, helping farming and guaranteeing the wellbeing of biological systems. Their transitory excursions range mainlands, interfacing unique environments and impacting biodiversity across tremendous scenes. Perceiving the many-sided connections swallows fashion inside biological systems highlights the criticalness of our aggregate liability in safeguarding their essentialness.

Difficulties to Swallow Populaces:

Swallow species face a variety of difficulties that undermine their populaces. Natural surroundings misfortune because of urbanization, farming strengthening, and deforestation upsets their settling locales. Environmental change adjusts movement examples and impacts the accessibility of bugs, affecting their food sources. Pesticide use and contamination further undermine their wellbeing and conceptive achievement. These difficulties are not separated; they are interconnected strings woven into the more extensive texture of natural debasement.

The Interconnected Web: A Call for Aggregate Liability:

The difficulties going up against swallow species are not elite to these avian occupants. They mirror the more extensive issues of territory annihilation, environmental change, and natural irregularity that influence the whole planet. Accentuating aggregate liability is an affirmation that our activities, both independently and all in all, add to the difficulties looked by swallows and other untamed life. It is an acknowledgment of the interconnected snare of life and the common obligation to defend the variety and imperativeness of our environments.

The Job of People:

People hold monstrous power in molding the direction of ecological protection. Each activity, from making bird-accommodating spaces in our nurseries to decreasing our biological impression, adds to the protection of swallow territories. By bringing issues to light in our networks, partaking in resident science drives, and settling on earth cognizant decisions, people become impetuses for change. The aggregate liability starts with individual decisions that focus on the prosperity of these essential bird species.

Networks as Stewards of Nature:

Networks assume a critical part as stewards of nature. The common spaces we possess, whether metropolitan or provincial, can be planned and figured out how to oblige the requirements of swallows. Drives, for example, local area drove preservation projects, the foundation of untamed life amicable areas, and the assurance of mutual green spaces highlight the aggregate liability of networks in establishing conditions that help swallow populaces.

Hierarchical and Legislative Commitments:

Associations and legislative bodies bear a significant obligation in establishing strategies and drives that focus on ecological protection. By putting resources into natural surroundings conservation, executing feasible land-use practices, and controlling the utilization of pesticides, they can essentially add to the prosperity of swallow species. Coordinated effort between preservation associations, administrative organizations, and examination establishments intensifies the effect of drives pointed toward safeguarding these crucial bird species.

Worldwide Coordinated effort:

The transitory idea of swallows rises above topographical limits, stressing the requirement for worldwide cooperation in preservation endeavors. Shared transitory courses require worldwide collaboration to address difficulties along their excursions. Joint exploration drives, transboundary protection arrangements, and the trading of best practices become fundamental parts of the aggregate liability that reaches out past individual countries.

Instructive Drives for People in the future:

Imparting a feeling of obligation and natural stewardship in people in the future is foremost. Instructive drives that coordinate natural training into educational programs, advance outside growth opportunities, and connect with understudies in involved protection exercises support an age that qualities and comprehends the significance of safeguarding biodiversity. By outfitting the young with information and encouraging an association with nature, we guarantee that the tradition of aggregate liability perseveres.

The Force of Support:

Support arises as a powerful device in preparing aggregate liability. People, people group, and associations can advocate for strategy changes that focus on natural protection. By voicing concerns, taking part out in the open talk, and considering leaders responsible, advocates add to molding approaches that address the main drivers of difficulties looked by swallow species.

Supportable Practices for Long haul Effect:

The quintessence of aggregate liability lies in the reception of reasonable practices that have an enduring effect. From economical agribusiness and dependable pesticide use to the protection of regular environments, these practices line up with our comprehension that the decisions today resound through the ages to come. Maintainability turns into a common obligation to guaranteeing the essentialness of swallow species and the biological systems they possess.